P9-DGC-420

The Apache

Indians of North America

Heritage Edition

◀ **Indians** ▶
◀ of **North** ▶
◀ **America** ▶

Heritage Edition

◀ Indians ▶
◀ of North ▶
◀ America ▶

The Apache

Michael E. Melody

With additional
text written by
Paul Rosier

Foreword by
Ada E. Deer
University of Wisconsin-Madison

CHELSEA HOUSE
PUBLISHERS
A Haights Cross Communications ◀ Company ®
Philadelphia

Cover: Apache warrior's cloak, Smithsonian Institution, Washington, D.C.

CHELSEA HOUSE PUBLISHERS

VP, New Product Development Sally Cheney
Director of Production Kim Shinners
Creative Manager Takeshi Takahashi
Manufacturing Manager Diann Grasse

Staff for THE APACHE

Executive Editor Lee Marcott
Editor Christian Green
Production Editor Bonnie Cohen
Photo Editor Sarah Bloom
Series and Cover Designer Keith Trego
Layout EJB Publishing Services

Original edition first published in 1989.

A Haights Cross Communications ✦ Company ®

First Printing

9 8 7 6 5 4 3 2 1

Library of Congress Cataloging-in-Publication Data

 The Apache / Michael E. Melody ; with additional text
written by Paul Rosier.— Heritage ed.
     p. cm. — (Indians of North America)
 Rev. ed. of: The Apache / Michael E. Melody. New York : Chelsea House
Publishers, c1989.
 Includes bibliographical references and index.
 ISBN 0-7910-8597-X (hard cover)
 1. Apache Indians—Juvenile literature. I. Melody, Michael Edward. II. Rosier,
Paul. III. Melody, Michael Edward. Apache. IV. Title. V. Indians of North America
(Chelsea House Publishers)
 E99.A6M46 2005
 979.004'9725—dc22

                              2005009889

Contents

Foreword

Ada E. Deer

American Indians are an integral part of our nation's life and
history. Yet most Americans think of their Indian neighbors
as stereotypes; they are woefully uninformed about them as
fellow humans. They know little about the history, culture, and
contributions of Native people. In this new millennium, it is
essential for every American to know, understand, and share in
our common heritage. The Cherokee teacher, the Mohawk
steelworker, and the Ojibwe writer all express their tribal heritage while living in mainstream America.

The revised INDIANS OF NORTH AMERICA series, which
focuses on some of the continent's larger tribes, provides the
reader with an accurate perspective that will better equip
him/her to live and work in today's world. Each tribe has a
unique history and culture, and knowledge of individual
tribes is essential to understanding the Indian experience.

Prior to the arrival of Columbus in 1492, scholars estimate the Native population north of the Rio Grande ranged from seven to twenty-five million people who spoke more than three hundred different languages. It has been estimated that ninety percent of the Native population was wiped out by disease, war, relocation, and starvation. Today there are more than 567 tribes, which have a total population of more than two million. When Columbus arrived in the Bahamas, the Arawak Indians greeted him with gifts, friendship, and hospitality. He noted their ignorance of guns and swords and wrote they could easily be overtaken with fifty men and made to do whatever he wished. This unresolved clash in perspectives continues to this day.

A holistic view recognizing the connections of all people, the land, and animals pervades the life and thinking of Native people. These core values—respect for each other and all living things; honoring the elders; caring, sharing, and living in balance with nature; and using not abusing the land and its resources—have sustained Native people for thousands of years.

American Indians are recognized in the U.S. Constitution. They are the only group in this country who has a distinctive *political* relationship with the federal government. This relationship is based on the U.S. Constitution, treaties, court decisions, and attorney-general opinions. Through the treaty process, millions of acres of land were ceded *to* the U.S. government *by* the tribes. In return, the United States agreed to provide protection, health care, education, and other services. All 377 treaties were broken by the United States. Yet treaties are the supreme law of the land as stated in the U.S. Constitution and are still valid. Treaties made more than one hundred years ago uphold tribal rights to hunt, fish, and gather.

Since 1778, when the first treaty was signed with the Lenni-Lenape, tribal sovereignty has been recognized and a government-to-government relationship was established. This concept of tribal power and authority has continuously been misunderstood by the general public and undermined by the states. In a series of court decisions in the 1830s, Chief Justice John Marshall described tribes as "domestic dependent nations." This status is not easily understood by most people and is rejected by state governments who often ignore and/or challenge tribal sovereignty. Sadly, many individual Indians and tribal governments do not understand the powers and limitations of tribal sovereignty. An overarching fact is that Congress has plenary, or absolute, power over Indians and can exercise this sweeping power at any time. Thus, sovereignty is tenuous.

Since the July 8, 1970, message President Richard Nixon issued to Congress in which he emphasized "self-determination without termination," tribes have re-emerged and have utilized the opportunities presented by the passage of major legislation such as the American Indian Tribal College Act (1971), Indian Education Act (1972), Indian Education and Self-Determination Act (1975), American Indian Health Care Improvement Act (1976), Indian Child Welfare Act (1978), American Indian Religious Freedom Act (1978), Indian Gaming Regulatory Act (1988), and Native American Graves Preservation and Repatriation Act (1990). Each of these laws has enabled tribes to exercise many facets of their sovereignty and consequently has resulted in many clashes and controversies with the states and the general public. However, tribes now have more access to and can afford attorneys to protect their rights and assets.

Under provisions of these laws, many Indian tribes reclaimed power over their children's education with the establishment of tribal schools and thirty-one tribal colleges. Many Indian children have been rescued from the foster-care system. More tribal people are freely practicing their traditional religions. Tribes with gaming revenue have raised their standard of living with improved housing, schools, health clinics, and other benefits. Ancestors' bones have been reclaimed and properly buried. All of these laws affect and involve the federal, state, and local governments as well as individual citizens.

Tribes are no longer people of the past. They are major players in today's economic and political arenas; contributing millions of dollars to the states under the gaming compacts and supporting political candidates. Each of the tribes in INDIANS OF NORTH AMERICA demonstrates remarkable endurance, strength, and adaptability. They are buying land, teaching their language and culture, and creating and expanding their economic base, while developing their people and making decisions for future generations. Tribes will continue to exist, survive, and thrive.

Ada E. Deer
University of Wisconsin–Madison
June 2004

1

The Game of Survival

Long ago, before humans inhabited the earth, huge beasts stalked the land, and vast serpents slithered across it. These creatures were always famished, so they fed on small birds as well as on wolves, rabbits, and squirrels. The small creatures tried to flee, but because the world was shrouded in eternal darkness they could not see where they were going.

One day all the creatures—large and small—met on Mescal Mountain, which rose above the desert in what is now New Mexico. A debate concerning daylight began. The monsters, beasts, and serpents wanted the world to remain dark so they could continue to pursue the smaller animals, who, of course, favored daylight. After a lengthy quarrel, the two sides agreed to settle the issue with a game. Each side dug many holes in the ground and hid sticks in one of them. The other side then tried to guess which hole held the sticks. If they guessed correctly they gained possession of the sticks. The side that won all the sticks would be declared the champion and would slaughter the losers.

The contest was close. First the small creatures—led by the birds—forged ahead, collecting several sticks. Then the beasts rallied. Eventually, the birds were left with only a single stick and faced a terrible loss. One hope remained. At the start of the game, a large bird, Turkey, had placed some sticks in his moccasin and wandered off to nap. Now the other birds ran to awaken him. Turkey brought his sticks and joined the game. A deft player, he helped the birds win back many sticks. They even took some held by the beasts and moved into the lead. Soon the beasts were down to only a handful, and, to their amazement, the sky, which had always been pitch black, filled with light. Wren, a small songbird, chirped, "Daybreak is coming! Daybreak is coming!" The beasts lost their last stick, and the birds started to kill them.

In their excitement the birds set upon one of the most fearsome beasts, Giant. They removed arrows from their quivers and shot at him, but they failed to pierce his heart. Giant still lived. Suddenly, one of the beasts, Lizard, changed sides and came to the aid of the birds. He knew that Giant's heart was lodged in the underside of his foot. He aimed an arrow there, and at last Giant was slain. The other beasts panicked and fled, chased by the birds. They shot arrows at Snake, but he slithered into a crevice on a cliff where they could not reach him. Thus, though no giants inhabit the earth today, the desert is filled with snakes.

This story—which pits large animals in a violent contest against smaller ones and whose outcome seems a matter of sheer luck—provides many clues to the culture from which it originated: that of the Apaches. These people inhabited the Great Plains and the deserts of Texas, New Mexico, and Arizona, in what is now called the American Southwest.

This region has a harsh and changeable climate. Fierce winds whip year-round over the level acreage. In the summer,

The Apaches were fierce warriors and defended their land from all intruders. Though the Spanish attempted to settle in Arizona, the Apaches resisted and never allowed them to establish a town north of Tucson. Shown here is an Apache weapon of war: a shield painted by Geronimo in the early twentieth century, while he lived on Fort Sill Reservation in Oklahoma.

they gust up from the south with the intensity of flames. Autumn winds, often from the southeast, bring warmer air. In the winter, chilly winds funnel down from the north. The Apaches weathered these extremes by living as nomads. Their only permanent home was the land itself, which they roamed as the seasons changed and as the animals they hunted—deer, elk, antelope, and buffalo—sought out comfortable temperatures and grassy places where they could graze.

As the legend of the birds and the beasts attests, the stark environment of the plains taught the Apaches to view life as a contest—fought against the elements and against other humans. The various Apache groups generally stayed on peaceful terms with one another but made no effort to uphold peaceful relations with other Indians. The Apaches engaged in long-running feuds with the *Pawnee* and other Plains *tribes*: the *Pima, Papago,* and the *Sobaipuri.*

The Apaches, perhaps more than most other Indian groups, were warriors. They took up arms for many reasons—in disputes over trading, hunting, and territorial rights; to seek revenge; and in immediate retaliation for recently committed wrongs. Thus, the Apaches gained a reputation for being among the most warlike of Native American groups. Even their name conveys ferocity. *Apache* derives from *ápachu* and means "enemy"—in the language used by the Zuni, a sedentary southwestern tribe that traded with them in the sixteenth century. By 1598, *ápachu* was the term most commonly used by other Indian groups.

By the time white people arrived on their territory in the mid-1500s, the Apaches had hardened into talented and fearless warriors prepared to meet any intrusion with force. First, they clashed with Spanish *conquistadores*—or conquerors—who had many advantages over the Apaches, including horses and firearms. The Apaches developed a taste for both items and often traded for or stole them. The Spaniards did not venture far into Apache territory, but in the seventeenth, eighteenth, and nineteenth centuries the culture they perpetuated in Mexico steadily encroached on Apache lands. In the 1820s, when Mexico shook off its colonial yoke and became an independent republic, its citizens often skirmished with the Apaches, who sought to protect their land, their buffalo, and their practice of raiding for food, equipment, and human

Cochise, a Chiricahua Apache, was one of several well-known Apache chiefs who resisted the intrusion of white settlers into their territory. After his band was accused of stealing cattle by an Arizona rancher, Cochise launched a twenty-five-year war between the Chiricahuas and the United States.

captives. Then, in the 1840s and 1850s, after Mexico ceded vast territory to the United States, the Apaches squared off against a new batch of intruders: American soldiers, gold prospectors, and settlers.

Fierce as the Apaches were, their entire population numbered only about five thousand and did not form a unified nation such as that of the *Lakota*. Nor did they have tribal leaders. Instead they broke down into much smaller units that lived, hunted, raided, and warred on their own. By the 1860s, most of these *bands*—which could include up to a hundred warriors—waged protracted battles against the U.S. Army and also against vigilantes, or loosely organized but heavily armed groups of civilians.

Atrocities abounded on both sides, as the Americans sought to subdue the Apaches and pin them within the margins of the land they had once roamed freely. Though badly overmatched, the Apaches held off the Americans until the late nineteenth century. Their war leaders—Mangas Coloradas, Cochise, Geronimo, and Victorio—rank among the most renowned Indians in American history.

In the end, the Apaches succumbed to the superior numbers and firepower of their adversaries. No Apache band was ever really conquered, but all eventually submitted and accepted the terms dictated by the white man. They laid down their arms, gave up their nomadic way of life, and moved onto *reservations*—mainly worthless tracts of land set aside by the U.S. government. There they have struggled since to subsist as farmers, ranchers, sheepherders, and businesspeople, while retaining their ancestral language, customs, and beliefs.

Contemporary Apaches keep alive the memory of their ancestors, products and custodians of the land who fought fiercely to maintain their independence against overwhelming odds. Their story is one of the tragedies of American history, but it is filled with incidents of triumph and lit throughout with heroism and pride.

2

Origins
and
Habits

Originally, the Apaches belonged to the *Athapaskan* federation, a
people who inhabited the region of the North American continent in and around present-day Alaska and northwestern Canada.
No one knows exactly why the Apaches left this territory, nor exactly
when, but it is certain that between A.D. 1000 and 1500 this group
joined a mass southward migration of Athapaskans who had broken
away from the larger group.

Journeying south along the eastern edge of the Rocky
Mountains, the Athapaskans proceeded into the western part of the
Great Plains—the present-day states of Colorado, New Mexico, and
Utah. By the 1400s signs of Apache life appeared in various pockets
of a vast territory that covered much of the American Southwest.
This region stretched some eight hundred miles north to south
(from Kansas down to northern Mexico) and some two hundred to
four hundred miles east to west (from Oklahoma to Arizona). It

Chiricahua Apaches lived in southeastern Arizona, in a rugged land filled with jagged rock formations, ponderosa pines, and Douglas firs. Shown here is a view from the Chiricahua Mountains, looking toward New Mexico.

encompassed parts of Texas and Colorado and all of New Mexico.

Because the Apaches were nomads, ready on short notice to take all their belongings and move to new campsites, they lived in small groups that were mobile and could easily settle in new places. Each of these groups, formed from a network of blood relatives, staked out its own territory and became self-sufficient.

During wartime, groups merged into larger units—several hundred people strong—called bands. These bands took on the characteristics of tribes, with their own language, customs, and organization. Today, the bands are identified by Spanish names given them by the first white people with whom they came into contact.

The bands can be distinguished best by geography. The easternmost Apache group was the Kiowa-Apaches, who blended in with the Kiowa nation in modern-day Kansas and Oklahoma. Next came the Lipans, who lived in the lower Rio Grande valley in New Mexico and Mexico and ranged toward the Texas coast. Farther west were the Jicarillas. They lived in northern New Mexico and southern Colorado and camped and hunted along the Rio Grande, near modern-day Santa Fe. The Mescaleros inhabited New Mexico, ranged from the Rio Grande in the west to the Pecos River area in southwestern Texas (near the town of Pecos), and hunted and camped in northern Mexico. Farther west, in New Mexico and also in Arizona, lived the Chiricahuas. Finally, there were the Western Apaches, who comprised five major subgroups—the White Mountain Apaches, the San Carlos Apaches, the Cibecue Apaches, the Southern Tontos, and the Northern Tontos—all of whom resided in east-central Arizona, just above the Mexican border.

Despite these geographical distinctions, the various Apache bands viewed themselves as a single, related people. The Apaches called themselves *N'de, Dinï, Tindé,* or *Indé*—all derived from the term *tinneh,* meaning "the people" superior to all other humans, whom they regarded as members of an inferior species.

The various Apache groups were linked by their physical appearance. Most Apache men were of medium stature, thin and well muscled, and had enormous stamina. Warriors could run fifty miles without stopping to rest and were so swift they could outdistance mounted troops. This uncanny ability would play a significant role in their encounter with the U.S. Army. Most Apache women, several inches shorter than the men, were slender and lithe.

The dwellings built by the different Apache groups were also similar. The Kiowas, Jicarillas, and some Chiricahuas lived in *tepees*, or cone-shaped dwellings covered with animal hides. Most Apaches, however, lived in *wickiups*—circular or oval huts made of brush, with earthen floors scooped out to enlarge the living area. As the seasons changed, so did the wickiup's outer coverings. In summer, leafy branches were draped over the dwelling; in winter, animal hides, expertly tanned, provided insulation. For added warmth, the Apaches burned a fire on the earthen floor (if the hut was big enough), and smoke escaped through a small hole in the roof.

In any case, these homes were temporary—suitable for a people whose lives followed the pattern of the seasons. The Chiricahuas placed their wickiups close together and burned them in preparation for their winter migration, when they traveled far into the highlands—lush hills or mountains whose peaks rose toward the warming rays of the sun. In summer they found cool relief in shady stands of cottonwood trees, whose roots drew nourishment from the creeks that snaked through this mostly barren area. The Apaches were also careful to build sites that could easily be defended against attackers.

The dry climate of the Southwest dictated the clothing worn by the Apaches. Women wore skirts; men wore *breechcloths*. Both items have been described by Ralph Ogle in *Federal Control of the Western Apache*: "The breechcloth was about two yards long. It passed between the legs and hung over the belt in front and behind, the rear part almost reaching the ground. A common buckskin skirt was composed of two buckskins hung over a belt, one in front and the other behind in the form of a kilt. The edges of the skirt were cut in deep fringe." Men and women alike wore knee-high moccasins whose folds served as pockets. The soles, which had to be durable, were made from undressed hides, and the toes were upturned. These unique shoes caused another Indian people, the Comanches, to refer to the Apaches as *Tá-ashi*, or "Turned-up."

Apaches were not sedentary people; they were always on the go and because of this they lived in temporary dwellings called wickiups—circular or oval huts made of brush, with earthen floors.

The climate also influenced the Apache diet. Precipitation was scant in this region. A year's rainfall seldom surpassed twenty inches and often did not reach ten. Consequently, little vegetation grew in the plains. Some grasses thrived, but only because they were hardy enough to withstand the climatic extremes of the sudden storms, long droughts, and the fires that sometimes seared the land.

The Apaches seldom farmed, not only because the climate discouraged it but also because they were frequently on the move and unlikely to linger long enough in one place to nurture their crops. Some Apaches did cultivate the land, however. The Western Apaches grew maize (corn), beans, and squash and even remained near their crops for part of the year. Still, the harvest provided only 20 percent of their diet.

The Apaches fared better as hunters. Game was plentiful in the Southwest, and most bands included meat in their diet.

They savored the meat of antelope, deer, hare, and even rodents, which they hunted skillfully with bows and arrows. The Kiowa, Lipan, and Chiricahua bands all hunted buffalo and prepared its meat in many ways—boiled, baked, roasted, even raw. They set aside some of the flesh to be dried on racks, then eaten as jerky. Buffalo blood thickened stews, soups, and puddings. The Apaches used more than just the flesh of the animals they killed. Buffalo hide could be sewn into sturdy bags, moccasins, robes, and more. Women made blankets and scarves from buffalo hide, and warriors made shields, lariats, and cords.

Women contributed to the food supply by gathering fruits, vegetables, roots, and nuts that grew wild, including strawberries, grapes, and mulberries; onions, potatoes, and mesquite beans; piñon nuts and walnuts; and sunflower seeds and acorns. These foodstuffs constituted a major portion of the diet: 40 percent among the Western Apaches, the most agricultural of the bands.

One method of obtaining food was raiding, which the Apaches viewed as a life-sustaining enterprise, like hunting and food gathering. They raided primarily to steal food, preferably livestock, but they also made off with weapons, supplies, and children, whom they accepted into the band and raised as their own. Before the Spaniards introduced horses to the Apaches in the sixteenth century, raiding warriors traveled by foot. Their depredations were the major cause of discord between Apache bands and other Indians and would later cause friction with non-Indian settlers.

The Apaches developed a distinct social organization. Its fundamental unit was the family. Unlike contemporary American households, which usually consist only of parents and children, Apache home life was centered on the extended family. Its members included the various blood relations of the parents and their offspring—grandparents and grandchildren, cousins, aunts and uncles, nephews and nieces.

In Apache culture these persons constituted a kind of miniature society that lived in adjacent wickiups, shared tasks such as hunting and gathering, and assisted each other in times of stress. An important figure was the mother-in-law, who supervised much social activity. Sons-in-law, for instance, brought her game they had killed. She cooked and apportioned it to others in the group.

Marriage was a crucial event because it redistributed males among different families. In the Jicarilla culture, when a couple decided to marry, the suitor's relatives bestowed gifts upon the relatives of his intended bride. In all the bands, the relatives had to agree to any marriage. Once the match was approved, the wedding took place. It involved little ceremony. A large basin made of buffalo hide was carried to a secluded place and filled with fresh water. The bride and groom stepped into it, held hands, and awaited the appearance of both sets of parents, who had to acknowledge the matrimony. Afterward the party walked together to the bride's camp and joined a public dance.

The wedded couple took up residence near the wife's relatives, and the husband provided for them and fulfilled their wishes. This relationship continued even if the wife died. On such an occasion, the widower mourned for a year, then married one of his wife's sisters or cousins. If the husband died first, his widow was expected to marry one of his brothers or cousins.

Despite the close bonds formed between spouses and their in-laws, the Apaches allowed for divorce. Incompatibility and infidelity could end a marriage, as could laziness, bickering, and jealousy. If a married woman misbehaved, her husband left the camp. In the event her family recognized him as a good provider, they would make an effort to keep him happy by straightening out his wife. If her family had no use for him, they drove him away.

As we might expect from a group that so highly valued the wife's family, the Apaches were matrilineal—that is, they traced

Apaches were matrilineal, that is, they traced their descent through their mother's family. These family groups, known as clans, were typically named after a nearby natural feature, such as hills, water, or rocks. Shown here is an Apache mother with her child, who is inside a cradleboard.

their descent through their mother. In some groups, families connected by common ancestors constituted a *clan*. The Western Apaches, for example, comprised sixty clans, most named for some natural feature of the landscape they inhabited. Clan names included Water at the Foot of Hill People, Between Two Hills People, White Water People, and In the Rocks People. Members of the same clan could not marry each other.

Within the family, tasks were generally divided along gender lines, with some crossing over. Hunting, for example, was a male activity, but Lipan women helped track down rabbits and antelope, and men in the various tribes sometimes helped pick berries and other fruits. Similarly, women tanned hides, but men assisted with large or heavy skins, such as those removed from the carcasses of slain buffalo and antelope. Women raised children, but fathers and male relatives often pitched in. Sewing, however, was strictly women's work, as was gathering brush for fires and cooking. Men repaired their own hunting weapons adeptly, and Apache warriors were known for fashioning some of the finest arrows, arrowheads, and lances ever produced by American Indians.

When several extended families merged, they formed a local group. Day to day, the group unit functioned like the extended families and was led by the male heads of each. When a serious issue—such as dwindling resources or enemy threats—faced the group, the family heads convened in a council that discussed the problem and planned a strategy. The council itself was led by an inner circle composed not only of family heads but also of other men noted for bravery, wealth, or wisdom. The most dominant man among those in the inner circle served as the group's top leader.

Local groups were not always large enough or strong enough to solve all the problems that faced them. Thus, they merged to form yet a larger union, the band, which usually contained between two hundred to three hundred people. It too had an inner council, and its members were the main leaders of the individual groups. The most respected of these leaders dominated the band, just as the local leaders dominated the groups and the family head dominated the extended family.

The band council probably functioned differently from the group council. It seems that the local-group council focused on such everyday matters as locating ideal places to hunt, whereas the band council was more concerned with organizing raiding parties and planning for war. Both councils, however, worked democratically. All members expressed opinions and tried to achieve a consensus, so that everyone shared in the final decision and helped carry it out. Even a towering figure such as Cochise, the nineteenth-century Chiricahua chief, consulted with his council before guiding his band into action.

Leaders had many responsibilities. They settled disputes between competing families and persons and made sure that the band or group worked harmoniously to hunt and gather food. Their most important task was giving advice. Indeed the Chiricahua word for leader, *nantà*, translates as "he who talks or advises." One twentieth-century Apache, quoted in Morris Opler's *An Apache Life-Way*, enumerated the qualities of the ideal leader:

> The leader is supposed to talk to his people. He is supposed to be sympathetic and tell them how to live, sympathetic in the sense of giving out horses and valuables to those who need them. The leader is supposed to give something to eat to everyone who comes around [in need]. He has control in time of war. You can't disobey him. The leader advises people to help the unfortunate, to give to those whose luck is bad. He advises against fights in the camps; he doesn't want any quarrels within the group. He advises the people to be on the lookout all the time. He may request that a ceremony be performed by a shaman [a healer] for the benefit of the men during a raid. If the leader is advised by the shaman as a result of such a ceremony to do this or that, he carries out what the power tells him to do. A man must be wealthy and have a big following to be a chief.

An Apache leader, then, had to possess many qualities— wealth, wisdom, sympathy, and strength. He had to speak well but also be willing to listen. He had to reach the right decision and command enough loyalty to enforce it. Often chiefs acquired leadership through family connections. The brothers or sons of a leader had an inside track on acquiring the mantle themselves. Yet—as in other societies—being born into the right family was never enough. Ultimately, leaders rose to eminence by acclaim.

At least several times a week, the leader assembled his group and addressed it from a prominent place—atop a rock or hill. Even when there was little news to report, the leader kept in touch with his people and offered advice meant to improve their lives. In *The Social Organization of the Western Apache*, anthropologist Grenville Goodwin provides an example of a typical speech:

> Do not be lazy. Even if there is a deep canyon or a steep place to climb, you must go up it. Thus, it will be easy for you to [track down and kill] deer. If any of you go out hunting this morning . . . , look after yourselves [when] you are alone. When you trail deer you may step on a rock. If the rock slips from under you, you may fall and get hurt. If there is a thick growth of trees ahead of you, don't go in it. There might be a lion in a tree ready to attack you.

In addition to advising the men on hunting methods, leaders took charge of the riskier business of raiding. Raids were staged by warriors who volunteered for the assignment, which was considered a privilege. If the attack was successful—that is, if the men made off with plunder (livestock and weapons) and no Apache lives were lost—the warriors usually held a feast and distributed some of the booty among the rest of the group.

An even more dangerous enterprise was warfare, which for centuries remained a crucial part of Apache existence. Most battles were undertaken to avenge the death of group members, who usually were killed during raids. The slain warrior's family led the way during battle. Costumed dancers called on other warriors, outside the family, to join the expedition. The head of the aggrieved family acted as leader, though he consulted with other men and might even submit to the authority of another, more respected leader. Before men departed to engage in battle, the community summoned the assistance of divine spirits by performing a dance in which the men took the part of *Child of the Water* and the women took the part of *White-painted Woman,* two mythological figures said to have founded the Apache nation. Anyone whom they opposed was considered a monster and the enemy of all human life. The dance reminded warriors that they sallied forth to engage no mere opponents but the would-be destroyers of their entire blessed race.

During peacetime, the Apaches lived a regulated existence. They had no laws, judges, police, or jails, but they obeyed a code of honor passed on from one generation to the next. As a twentieth-century Apache explained to researcher Morris Opler:

> Good conduct is the result of obeying the customs, and it is up to the person. . . . A man would come to a bad end in the old days [if] he violated the customs. . . . If you obey all the rules, you get along all right. . . . But if a person doesn't take hold of the customs, if he cuts loose, if he doesn't treat other people right, he has no chance. Then the others do not help him. He is alone. He is bound to come to a bad end and perhaps be killed. A person just has to observe certain things. They aren't laws—they are so strong we don't need laws.

3

Power
and
Portent

Rules of conduct invariably rest on a deep foundation of spiritual belief. Such was the case with the Apaches. Edward Curtis states in *The North American Indian*, a multivolume work published in 1930, that "the Apache is inherently devoutly religious; his life is completely molded by his religious beliefs. From his morning prayers to the rising sun, through the hours, the days and the months—throughout life itself—every act has some religious significance."

The Apaches did not build religious institutions, but they incorporated spirituality into their everyday life. The nineteenth-century Chiricahua leader Geronimo, who also served the role of healer, explained his band's religious attitude in *Geronimo's Story of His Life*:

> We had no churches, no religious organizations, no sabbath day, no holidays, and yet we worshipped. Sometimes the whole tribe would assemble to sing and pray; sometimes in a smaller number, perhaps

only two or three. . . . Sometimes we prayed in silence; sometimes each one prayed aloud; sometimes an aged person prayed for all of us.

According to the Apaches, the universe was imbued with *power*, which they regarded as a spiritual substance or cosmic force. Every object, idea, and person contained elements of power; it was present everywhere, like air. Sometimes power served good purposes, breathing vitality into living things. Yet, power was equally responsible for disease and death, and good power could degenerate into bad. Though invisible, power could be discerned easily and in a variety of ways. Someone who experienced muscle tremors, for instance, took them as physical evidence of power. Dreams also conveyed power. Power could be obtained more directly on occasions in which it sought out human contacts, who became the vehicle of its wishes.

These encounters between a person and power could be dangerous and often put the person to a test. An Apache quoted by Morris Opler described possible reactions to such a meeting:

I might reply to the power when it comes, "I'm a poor fellow, and there are many other people here good enough for that, let me alone. I don't want your ceremony!" . . . It is said that some fellows have done that. They claim it is more dangerous to take it than to refuse it sometimes. They say some power might help you nicely for several years and then begin a lot of trouble. You might have to sacrifice your friends. Then if you refuse you might get killed yourself. But, if I am not afraid and am interested in this power and this ceremony, I will go up [the mountain] the next morning. Then it will appear in the form of a person or as a spirit. "Well," it will say, "you will be a shaman and have power from the sun."

After making its presence known by speech, power later appeared in human form and spoke to the recipient. If he or she agreed to accept the offered power, then it revealed the details of a ceremony that only it could authorize.

Apache religious ceremonies often involve dancing. Shown here is a group of Apaches participating in the Gaan dance, which honors the mountain spirits and is performed by men who impersonate these spirits by painting their bodies and wearing black masks and headdresses.

The goodwill of power was cultivated in ceremonies supervised by religious figures—*shamans* and priests. Shamans, older men and sometimes women, rose to eminence by displaying unique spiritual gifts, especially the ability to communicate with supernatural beings. Hence, they served as mediums, conveying the hidden wishes of the sacred forces. Priests arrived at their post more formally, through inheritance and the diligent study of standard ritual knowledge taught by their elders. Instead of giving voice to the desires of the gods, these religious men functioned as intermediaries between the divine will and the mortal population.

Power, an elusive substance, freely defied mortal attempts

to harness it, especially if a shaman ran afoul of it. As one Apache has put it: "The old people say that a shaman often falls out with his own power. Many stories have been told about that, all of them true. After many years, the power will ask some shamans to sacrifice some of their best friends or the very ones they love best in the family."

Power could also render useful services. It could weaken enemies, protect groups from attack, even ward off arrows and bullets. Power was said to enable shamans to locate missing objects, root out hidden adversaries, and control the water supply and other natural phenomena. Its most beneficial service was allowing shamans to diagnose and cure illness.

This was done in ceremonies that, like other Apache activities, acknowledged their closeness to nature. Many Apache rituals, for example, involved pollen. Pollen represented the life force, fertility, and beauty. In the healing ceremony, it represented health, the condition that the patient sought to recapture.

The healing ceremony began with an event attended by the patient, his or her relatives, and other members of the local group. The sufferer initiated the proceedings by formally approaching the healer with a request for aid. He then spoke the name of the shaman and his family and demonstrated his respect and faith by marking the healer with pollen. Next he traced a cross on the shaman's right foot, sprinkled other parts of his body with pollen, and drew a second cross, this time on the left foot. Sometimes, the supplicant also gave the healer gifts, even a single cigarette. By accepting the present, or smoking the cigarette, the shaman indicated his willingness to take the case.

The shaman then took over. An Apache explained to Morris Opler what one such healer did:

> First he rolled a cigarette, blew smoke in the four cardinal directions—which were considered sacred—and said, "May it be well." Then he called upon his power. "This woman is in poor health. I want her to live. She has been searching for

Fringed and beaded bags, White Mountain Apache Cultural Center and Museum, Fort Apache, Arizona.

Basket with fringe, White Mountain Apache Cultural Center and Museum, Fort Apache, Arizona.

Saddlebags, White Mountain Apache Cultural Center and Museum, Fort Apache, Arizona.

Pitch-covered tus (water basket), White Mountain Apache Cultural Center and Museum, Fort Apache, Arizona.

Basket vase, White Mountain Apache Cultural Center and Museum, Fort Apache, Arizona.

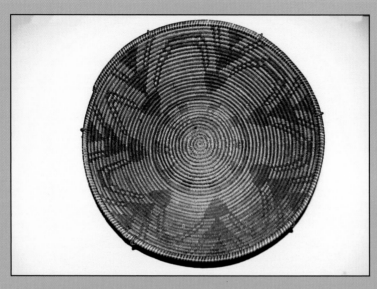

Flat basket, White Mountain Apache Cultural Center and Museum, Fort Apache, Arizona.

Flat basket, White Mountain Apache Cultural Center and Museum, Fort Apache, Arizona.

Flat basket, White Mountain Apache Cultural Center and Museum, Fort Apache, Arizona.

*D*esigns for twined baskets are also created by twisting the split strands of **squawberry** or **willow**, which are used for the wefts, to show the lighter inner surface or the outer reddish bark. The pattern shows in reverse on the interior of the basket. This technique is used on modern *táts'aa'* as well as *tús*.

Deep-twined basket, White Mountain Apache Cultural Center and Museum, Fort Apache, Arizona.

something good. This evening I hope that what is wrong with her will disappear and that she will have a good life. . . . You must do right now what you promised me to do. Your power must go into the life of this poor woman."

Next, the shaman explained the origin and meaning of this particular ceremony, and he and the sick person marked one another with pollen. The healer then sang and prayed to his power, who might inform him that he had correctly diagnosed the illness and should proceed with his cure.

The ceremony was repeated on four consecutive nights. It began at dark and continued until midnight, when everyone dined on food provided by the patient's relatives. At the conclusion of the fourth night, the healer sucked out poison supposedly planted in the patient by an evil shaman or *witch* and spat it into a fire. He then would impose restrictions on the patient, often dietary, such as a prohibition against eating liver. The healer might also give a protective charm to the suppliant.

Every Apache band, with the exception of the Kiowas, celebrated the Mountain Spirits, originally part of the religion practiced by the Pueblos, another southwestern people. The Mountain Spirits generally represented good power and could protect people from illness. They were invoked in a healing ceremony similar to the one described previously, except that it used *masked dancers.*

As with the ceremony previously described, the patient approached the shaman and formally presented his case. He also lavished gifts on the healer and marked him with pollen. By throwing himself on the mercy of the shaman, the patient sought his pity, the emotion that led the healer to salve the wound. If the shaman accepted the case, he selected four men to act as masked dancers and then painted them in an elaborate style. Meanwhile, the patient's relatives built a corral with a fire burning in the center and openings in the structure facing in each direction. The patient was then placed in the corral to await the dancers.

Drums sounded as the dancers approached from the east, trailing the shaman, who sang and danced as the troupe entered. He stepped toward the flame, circled it clockwise, then retraced his steps toward the east. The four dancers circled the fire four times, assumed positions of worship, and followed the shaman to the ailing suppliant, who daubed them with paint. Next the shaman approached the patient, asked where he hurt, and then directed the dancers to execute a series of steps four times. After the last series, the lead dancer ceremonially exhaled in every direction in order to blow the illness away. The other dancers did likewise, then left the corral.

This ceremony was repeated, with slight variations, for three more nights. On the second or third night, the healer might check the patient's progress. He pressed abalone—a mollusk with a spiral shell—against the patient's forehead. If the abalone stuck, his chances of recovery were good. If not, he faced prolonged illness. In either case, the ceremony continued for the full four nights. After a favorable prognosis, the shaman prescribed remedies. He might instruct the patient to avoid certain foods. He also warned the patient that if he violated these restrictions, disease would recur. If the outlook seemed bad, the shaman prayed for the afflicted person until he recovered. Sometimes this ceremony was performed on a larger scale to benefit the whole community.

Just as the Apaches believed in the life-force, so they believed that death held mysterious powers. When someone died, his or her relatives began a period of mourning. They wailed, cut their hair, and donned old clothing. Older relatives then prepared the corpse for burial. Some Apaches were afraid to touch dead bodies and enlisted strangers or captives to lay them to rest. Others enacted a burial ritual that could have originated no earlier than the mid-sixteenth century, when the Spaniards introduced the Apaches to horses. In this ritual, horses served as hearses. Relatives of the dead person loaded up a horse with the body of the dead person, along with his personal possessions, and led it away from the camp. They hid the dead person among crevices in the rocks, then destroyed most of the belongings, entombing the remainder much as the ancient Egyptians buried the dead along with their cherished goods. The burial party slew the horse and returned to camp, where they cleansed themselves and burned their ritual clothing.

According to Apache mythology, when someone died, his or her body released a spirit that was guided into the underworld by the ghosts of dead relatives. The Lipans, Jicarillas, and Western Apaches all believed the underworld consisted of two sections. One was a pleasant green place inhabited by the ghosts of virtuous people. The other was a barren place inhabited by the ghosts of witches.

To hasten the ghost's departure, living relatives conducted a formal funeral service. It had to be observed to the letter. Otherwise the ghost might decide to remain among the living and cause them harm. Even a ghost properly banished to the underworld might return to wreak sickness and death on the living. Thus, every effort was made to hold the dead at bay— even thinking about the dead, it was believed, encouraged ghosts to return. The relatives of the deceased isolated themselves for a while from the rest of the band and avoided social functions. An entire group might move camp because ghosts were thought to favor familiar places.

Nothing guaranteed that ghosts would remain in the underworld. Ghosts grew lonely there and longed for human company. They returned to find companions whom they could transport back with them. Thus, the Apaches believed that seeing a ghost doomed one to death. The ghosts of witches who had been exposed and burned alive were the most frightening of all. The Lipans, Jicarillas, and Chiricahuas also feared the ghosts of enemies. Ghosts chose nighttime to make their appearance. Sometimes they emerged from dreams or took the shape of owls or coyotes. Even steely Apache warriors quaked at the hooting of owls.

Not all rituals involved death and disease. Others, equally important, saluted life and health. One acknowledged the passage of young girls into puberty—the time when they were physically mature enough to bear children. This ceremony bespoke the Apache belief that the desire for fertility and beauty required a struggle with the earth, which yielded fruit only grudgingly, a desert world covered with the spiny skeletons of cacti and century plants—which flower only once, then die.

Two members of the band played important roles in this

The Slaying of the Monsters

Apache mythology describes the adventures of ancient gods, humans, and animals in order to explain the creation of the world and how it operates. Although each Apache tribe has its own unique stories, three culture heroes are common to all Apache mythology: White-painted Woman, *Killer of Enemies*, and Child of the Water.

One myth explains how, long ago, Child of the Water made the earth safe by killing four monsters who preyed on human beings. In the beginning, White-painted Woman and Killer of Enemies, who was either her brother or son, lived together on the earth. They were tormented by monsters, especially Owl-man Giant, who stole the deer meat shot with bow and arrow by Killer of Enemies. One day when White-painted Woman was praying for the monsters to leave them alone, the spirit known as *Life Giver* came to her in the form of rain and lightning and told her she would have a baby who would be called Child of the Water. The spirit warned White-painted Woman that she must protect the baby from Owl-man Giant. Through her cunning, White-painted Woman kept the child safe.

One day, while he was still a boy, Child of the Water told his mother that he was ready to leave her to kill the monsters. White-painted Woman fashioned him a wooden bow and grama-grass arrows and let him venture out to hunt deer with Killer of Enemies. After they had killed their first deer, ceremony. There was an attendant, an older woman, often with shamanistic gifts, who stayed with the initiate throughout the rite. A second functionary was the singer, usually an old man. Preparations for the girl's initiation began before the onset of menstruation. The girl's female relatives sewed and decorated an elaborate costume meant to duplicate the garb worn by White-painted Woman, the mythological figure said to have created the ceremony ushering girls into womanhood during her mortal time on earth.

The girl took on the role of White-painted Woman because

Owl-man Giant came to take the meat away. Child of the Water refused to give it up. The opponents agreed to a contest. Each would be allowed to shoot four arrows. Owl-man Giant was to shoot first but before he began, lightning flashed all around and a blue rock appeared at the feet of Child of the Water. The rock spoke, saying that Child of the Water should pick it up and use it as a charm. The boy did and waited for Owl-man Giant to shoot his arrows. They were made of sharp, large-pointed logs. The first arrow flew over Child of the Water's head. The second landed at his feet. The third and fourth missed him on either side.

Then it was Child of the Water's turn. Owl-man Giant wore four coats of flint to protect his chest and picked up a rock to try to deflect the arrows, as Child of the Water had done. But the first three arrows that Child of the Water shot knocked off a coat of flint, and the fourth pierced Owl-man Giant's heart.

Killer of Enemies and Child of the Water returned to White-painted Woman, who danced and sang with happiness. Child of the Water then went out again on further hunts. He killed the Buffalo Monster, then the Eagle Monster, and finally the Antelope Monster. The earth was now safe, and the human population began to grow. Thus, the Apaches regard Child of the Water as their divine ancestor.

The most important ritual among the Apaches is the puberty ceremony, which is depicted here on an animal hide. Known as *Na'ii'es* in Apache and the Sunrise Ceremony in English, the celebration traditionally takes place during the summer.

the Apaches associated the fertility of a budding woman with the fruitfulness of the earth. Thus, the initiate gained godlike power and blessed the Apache people by giving birth to new members and by linking the existing members with the procreative process. Before sunrise on the first day of the ceremony, an attendant dressed the young girl—referred to during the proceedings as White-painted Woman—in her finery and gave her precise instructions. Another attendant then initiated preparations for the construction of a tepee that duplicated the dwelling of White-painted Woman. This shelter was built at sunrise while songs were sung. When the singer named divine figures, the attendant cried out, simulating the cries emitted by White-painted Woman when Child of the Water returned victorious from his battle with Giant and other monsters.

As the first day ended, the attendant and the young girl entered the shelter and were marked with pollen. The attendant supervised a complex ritual. She placed an animal skin on the ground near the southeast corner of the tepee, where the girl knelt facing a basket filled with pollen and other objects. Next, the attendant offered the pollen to the four directions, painted the girl, and was painted by her in return. She then positioned her on the skin, face down, with her head pointing east, toward sunrise, and massaged her, praying the girl would be virtuous and mannerly. The girl rose, and the attendant painted four footprints of pollen on the animal skin. The girl then trod in these steps, again toward the east, which promised good health and luck.

This solemn ritual gave way to more public activities in the afternoon. There was dancing, and some people approached the girl to request that she help the ill because her emergent womanhood instilled her with healing powers. At night masked dancers appeared. They worshiped a campfire and sometimes circled and blessed the ceremonial tepee. They danced to drive away sickness, then to amuse and entertain the people gathered for the occasion. Inside the tepee, the singer performed songs meant to guide the young initiate into a long, successful life.

These proceedings continued for four days and nights. On the last night, the activities within the tepee lasted till dawn. When the sun rose, the singer sang four songs, faced east, and painted his own face and head. He then painted the girl. He sang once again and drew a sun symbol on his left palm, then pointed his palm toward the rising sun. As its first rays struck the girl, the singer rubbed his painted hand on her head, then gripped a brush made of an eagle feather and grama grass and

This 1955 photo shows Apache girls being sprinkled with pollen during the Sunrise Ceremony. This annual coming-of-age ritual lasts four days and four nights and involves dancing and sacred acts that enable the girls who participate to become women.

painted her head with white clay. He marked the onlookers with pollen and also marked ceremonial food brought before him. Everyone ate and the singer and girl left the tepee. She followed a path that was marked with pollen on an animal skin, then returned for the last time to the tepee, which was knocked down by others in the group. The assembly tossed presents in the air and children scrambled for them. The initiate and her female attendant retired from the group for four days of recovery. The girl returned to her parents' dwelling eligible for marriage.

An equivalent ritual celebrated the arrival of boys at the threshold of manhood, when they became warriors and were permitted to marry. Preparations began in boyhood with rigorous physical training supervised at first by the boy's father and male relatives, who ordered him to practice running and also to perform feats that tested his strength and endurance—all for the purpose of honing his battle skills. Before they became warriors, youngsters accompanied their elders on raids. This exposed them to the dangers of the life that awaited them.

Daily life included instruction from older men in the ways of war. As one Apache remembered:

> They told me to sleep in a place from which I could get to cover quickly. And they told me "even if it is a hot day, don't go to the deep shade. Go under a little bush in the open or under grass. The first place a Mexican or another Indian or a wild animal looks when it comes along is the shade, and there you are. If you are in the tall grass and hear something, just pick some grass up, hold it before you, and look through it. Then it will be hard to see you, especially from a distance. If you are out where the brush is heavy and you want to conceal yourself without moving, just take a branch which is to the right or left and pull it in front of you."

When a young man reached puberty, he was ready for his formal initiation. First he had to study a special sacred language composed of about eighty phrases. For example, the word for *heart* translated as "that by means of which I live," and the word for *pollen* meant "becoming life."

The Apaches carried out these and all such rituals as meticulously as possible, although they knew full well that there was no sure way of staving off ill fortune. When it arose, they usually placed the blame on witchcraft practiced by evil shamans. As one Apache explained to Morris Opler:

> There are lots of ways to [distinguish] a witch from a shaman, though most people who have much power will have both kinds [good and evil]. The truth is [that] a person is a shaman if he uses his power for good, and a witch if he uses

it for evil. You have to guess [which he is] by what happens; you have to use your own judgment. Therefore, there are a good many people who look at the same person differently.

The ambiguity, then, originated in the unpredictable nature of power itself, which could suddenly veer from good to evil, benefiting the group one day, plaguing it the next. Witchcraft was hard to detect because no one owned up to it. By definition, it unfolded secretly, and the community could only guess when it had been practiced. An Apache described some telltale signs to Morris Opler:

> Sometimes witching is done with hair or with a rib and hair done up in buckskin. This is their arrow. . . . They shoot these objects into the body of the one they are making sick. . . . Few shamans try to take objects out of a sick person's body which have been placed there through evil influence. It is dangerous and most shamans are afraid. Sometimes the glance, the thought, or the speech of a witch will cause evil influence. And a witch can often work through [obtaining] some part of the man whom it wants to harm, such as hair or nail parings.

The ability of witches to accomplish their evil purposes by a glance, speech, or even a thought, the Apaches believed, enabled them to defy detection and added to their power. Hence, Apaches remained on the alert for subtle clues to witchcraft. Strange behavior, for instance, was thought to identify a witch. If a shaman spoke or dressed oddly or employed unusual healing charms he might arouse suspicion.

Whenever the Apaches suspected a witch was among them, they turned to powerful shamans, for it was believed only they could neutralize or defeat witchcraft. During the healing ceremony, for instance, when shamans discerned the cause of illness, they lured the witch into a contest of good and evil. Once a witch came under suspicion the Apaches acted quickly, as one man explained to Opler:

They string the witch up by the wrists so his feet are off the ground. The witch has to tell whom he witched. The confession is good evidence. . . . They never let [him] go if they prove [he is wicked]. Then a fire is built under the witch, and he is burned. Burning destroys a witch's power for future harm, but what he has already accomplished is not undone. Witches do not [die] quickly; they keep on living a long time.

If these harsh methods sound familiar, it is because they resemble those employed by Christians in Europe and in the American colonies. In the fifteenth century, the Spanish Inquisition—the result of an effort to convert an entire nation to the Roman Catholic faith—resulted in mass burnings of alleged witches. Sometimes a hundred might be set ablaze in a one-day ceremony called an *auto-da-fe* (act of the faith). Just as the Apaches singled out people who used unusual charms—those who devised unique ways of healing—so some Christians pounced on people who dared to engage in scientific experiments that clashed with the teachings of the Roman Catholic Church. Protestants, too, executed witches. In 1692, twenty were hanged by Puritans in the colonial town of Salem, Massachusetts.

Europeans would have been appalled by the comparison of their own "civilized" culture to that of a "barbaric" Indian tribe. They might have bridled no less at the suggestion that they held beliefs as mysterious as the Apache belief in shamans and pollen. Yet their very different forms of faith would meet—and clash—in a dramatic episode that helped shape American history.

4

The First Strangers

In 1526, some three decades after Christopher Columbus and his crew first stumbled onto the North American continent, Charles V, the king of Spain, granted a charter to explorer Pánfilo de Narvaez, authorizing him to conquer and colonize a vast area of the New World. Narvaez left the port of Sanlucar in June 1527 with five ships and a crew of six hundred. The voyage across the Atlantic Ocean lasted almost a year, as storms blew the ships off course. Many men had deserted by the spring of 1528, when the expedition sailed up the Gulf of Mexico and anchored in Tampa Bay, near present-day St. Petersburg, Florida.

Narvaez ordered the ships to press on up the gulf, toward Mexico. He then disembarked with three hundred men, who traveled inland by foot in search of gold, which they believed existed abundantly in this unknown land. Instead they found Apalachee Indians, whose resentment of the intruders forced Narvaez to retreat. Decimated by malnutrition and disease, his forces struggled back to the coast, but when they arrived no ships lay at anchor. In panic, the Spaniards hastily chopped down trees and fashioned the trunks into planks, riveting them together with spurs they plucked off their boots. For sails and rigging they used horse hides. In short order they had five roughhewn boats. They set sail on a westward voyage along the Gulf Coast toward Mexico, but as they drew near the coast of what is now Galveston, Texas, a gale destroyed craft and crew.

Only four men survived: Álvar Núñez Cabeza de Vaca, Alonso del Castillo Maldonado, Andrés Dorantes de Carranco, and his black slave, Estevanico. They clambered ashore, where they were captured by Indians and held for six years. At last they escaped and struggled across the parched landscape of Texas, toward colonies in Mexico established by the Spanish some years earlier. Their trek took more than a year. On the way they encountered buffalo—the first Europeans to do so—and friendlier Indians (including Apaches). These peoples hailed the four foreigners as healers and traders, treated them like kings, and escorted them to their destination, Mexico City, in March 1536. The Spaniards had recently established a colony there after destroying the native *Aztec* culture.

Welcomed into this Spanish colony near the southern end of Mexico, Cabeza de Vaca and his companions regaled their countrymen with tales of their wanderings. They described the turquoise, buffalo-hide robes, and cotton blankets they had seen in the possession of Indians who had obtained them by trading with great cities to the north. The weary travelers described the gold and other precious metals they had seen. Finally, they told of seven rich cities whose walls glittered with emeralds. Cabeza de Vaca and the others had not actually seen these cities, but they had heard of them from the Indians they had met on their journey.

The account of the seven cities gripped the imagination of Mendoza, the viceroy, or top official, in Mexico, who fancifully connected it with a timeworn Spanish legend. The tale originated in the eighth century, when the Moors, a people from northern Africa, invaded the Iberian Peninsula and overran Spain and Portugal. The Moors, who practiced Islam, persecuted Spain's population of Roman Catholics. Led by seven bishops, some of the Catholics fled in boats that sailed westward into the uncharted and mysterious Ocean Sea (the Atlantic). Legend had it that these bishops discovered a lush island stocked with food and studded with jewels and gold. The bishops named this paradise *Antilla*, and each of the seven built his own city there.

In later centuries, Spanish adventurers set out for Antilla, but none found it, and its fabled cities remained shrouded in mystery. But Cabeza de Vaca's account meshed with the legend of the cities—even if he had traveled through a place no eighth-century Spaniards could ever have visited—and the viceroy of Mexico wanted to send an expedition north to find them. Mendoza tried to entice Cabeza de Vaca and the other survivors to head the expedition, but they all spurned the offer. The viceroy located another candidate, Friar Marcos de Niza, a well-traveled missionary. He had just arrived in the colony after seven years of traveling in Santo Domingo (today the Dominican Republic), Guatemala, and other distant places in the Southern Hemisphere. Friar Marcos, according to John Terrell's *Apache Chronicle*, "display[ed] a craving for adventure and sightseeing which challenged his love for his work as a missionary." He jumped at Mendoza's offer to set off in search of the seven lost cities. The viceroy sent a letter to the king of Spain requesting permission to employ Friar Marcos in this manner.

In September 1538, Mendoza received royal approval, and he instructed Marcos and his guide, the slave Estevanico, to proceed to the west coast of Mexico in the company of Francisco Vásquez de Coronado, who was headed there to assume his duties as governor of Nueva Galicia. The trio reached that province's capital, Compostela, in December. Friar Marcos and Estevanico then waited for the warmth of spring before resuming their journey.

March came and the travelers set off, heading north. Three weeks later, the pair reached the village of Vacapan, where the friar remained to celebrate Easter. He told Estevanico, who was not a Christian, to continue the journey and gave him precise instructions. Estevanico should proceed no farther than 50 or 60 leagues (about 150 miles). If he discovered something of importance, he was to send back a cross the length of his palm. If he found out something of great importance, the cross should be two palms long. If he stumbled on something truly extraordinary, he should send back a large cross.

Just before Easter, Estevanico and several Indian guides departed Vacapan. For nearly a week, Friar Marcos heard nothing. Then some of the advance party returned to the village bearing a mammoth cross and a message from Estevanico urging Friar Marcos to rendezvous with him. Before the friar left, another cross arrived. Marcos set off with a party of his own, but when he arrived at the appointed village, Estevanico was not there.

The slave had pressed ahead on his own. He had passed through numerous Apache camps, where he was welcomed grandly and then sent off in style, as described in *Apache Chronicle*: "Around his arms and legs were fastened gay feathers and jingling bells. He was followed by two Spanish greyhounds, and was accompanied by numerous attractive women who had been given him by the tribes through which he had passed, or whom he took of his own will."

The next phase of Estevanico's journey led him to what is now northwestern New Mexico, to the Zuni River and the city of Hawikuh, near present-day Gallup. Hawikuh was a *pueblo*, a village built of adobe, or clay, houses, and it may have been in existence for two hundred years. It was the home of the Zunis, a branch of the Pueblo Indians. Hawikuh was a remarkable place and must have seemed doubly so to an outlander gazing upon it for the first time. But it was not the glittering metropolis envisioned by Mendoza.

The Zunis seized Estevanico and locked him in a hut outside the city. Local leaders interrogated him for three days. Estevanico told them that white men were following close behind him and that they served a powerful lord. The leaders did not believe him but discerned that the slave represented a foreign people that sought to conquer them. The Zunis killed Estevanico, then diced his body into small pieces, which they distributed among their people as evidence that the strange man was mortal.

Soon after, Friar Marcos, following the trail of his slave, reached Hawikuh. He had learned of Estevanico's gruesome end and did not venture past the outskirts of the pueblo. He claimed the land for the Spanish king and then began the long and arduous journey back to the Spanish settlements of Mexico. He reached Compostela in June 1539 and gave an exaggerated account of his travels to Coronado, who left for Mexico City with the friar. Marcos repeated his fanciful account to Mendoza. He swore Hawikuh was bigger than Mexico City, saying that its surrounding landscape was rich and fertile and that precious minerals abounded—just as Mendoza had hoped. Rumors of the pueblo's riches spread rapidly through the colony. According to Frank Lockwood, author of *Pioneer Days in Arizona,* "Everyone believed his story and everyone took it for granted that these newly discovered cities were rich in minerals and precious stones." At last, it seemed, the seven fabled cities had been found.

Mendoza and Coronado, however, wanted to be sure before mounting an expedition. In September 1539, the viceroy ordered Captain Melchior Díaz, a trustworthy man, to duplicate the journey taken by Friar Marcos. Díaz returned with less encouraging news. He had questioned Indians who knew nothing of gold or other treasures. The friar, hearing of this report, attacked it vehemently and defended his own story so persuasively that Coronado believed him.

On February 23, 1540, Coronado departed from Compostela for Hawikuh with an expeditionary force that included some 250 horsemen, 70 foot soldiers, 300 Mexicans, and 1,000 Indian servants. This cumbersome army plodded across terrain unlike any Friar Marcos had described. It was not green, lush, or inviting but brown, barren, and hostile. Coronado had expected to feed his troops with fruits and vegetables clustered thickly on opulent vines. But nothing edible grew in this sterile desert. Short on food and sapped by the heat, his army sank into exhaustion.

On July 7, 1540, when Coronado drew near Cíbola (the Spanish name for Hawikuh), his men could barely shoulder their weapons. The commander sent peaceful messages to the Indians, who rejected his overtures. Coronado then stormed the pueblo. Weak as his soldiers were, their horses and gunpowder overwhelmed the Zunis, who defended themselves only with arrows, spears, and knives. Hawikuh fell, but Coronado's forces grumbled when they discovered no jewels, no gold, no riches of any kind. They loudly cursed Friar Marcos.

Coronado himself remained convinced, however, that treasures awaited them. He marched on to another pueblo. Again he found no riches. Nor at the next stop. The six cities all resembled Hawikuh: modest places with adobe houses inhabited by people who struggled to gather sufficient food, wove baskets out of desert grasses, and warmed themselves before open campfires built of brushwood. Still, Coronado pushed on. Friar Marcos' fantasy had become his own. He learned of a land to the north called Quivira, besotted with riches. Coronado rode toward it with thirty horsemen.

Once again their hopes were dashed, but Coronado encountered Apaches camped at the mouth of the Rio Grande. One of the Spaniards, Pedro de Castaneda, recorded his impressions of the Apaches. John Terrell cites them in *The Plains Apache*:

Apaches traded a number of goods, including baskets, jars, and bowls such as these, to the Pueblo Indians in return for vegetables, minerals, and ceramics. The Apaches would later trade their goods with the Spanish and acquire cows, muskets, and horses.

"They travel like the Arabs," Castaneda wrote, "with their tents and troops of dogs loaded with poles." The Apaches also seemed highly intelligent. "Although they conversed by means of signs they made themselves understood so well there was no need for an interpreter." Coronado himself characterized them as "gentle people, faithful in their friendships." They would not remain so.

At last, in the autumn of 1542, Coronado resigned himself to failure. He led the remnants of his troops back to Mexico City and reported to the viceroy. Then he stepped down as governor of Nueva Galicia and retired to the quiet solitude of his Mexican estate.

The Coronado expedition failed, but the hopes that gave rise to it—the dream of riches—continued to inspire Spaniards, and later Americans, as they aggressively and imperiously claimed the lands inhabited by North American

Indians. As the sixteenth-century conquistador Hernán Cortés once told Montezuma, the last of the Aztec rulers of Mexico, "We are troubled with a disease of the heart for which gold is the only remedy." During the next three hundred years, the gold disease would consume many of those who tried to oust the Apaches from their land.

When the first Spanish settlements appeared in the northern provinces of Mexico, the pioneers found the Apaches living there to be on peaceful terms with the Pueblo Indians, their neighbors and main trading partners. The Pueblos coveted all the items the Apaches produced from slain buffalo-robes, skins, dried meat (or jerky), and more. The Apaches willingly exchanged them for the corn, beans, calabash (a gourd whose hollow shell can be used as a vessel), cotton, and various minerals and ceramics available from the Pueblos.

This thriving commerce was disrupted by the Spaniards, who beat the Pueblos into submission and grabbed their goods. Nonetheless, the Apaches remained on amicable terms with the Spanish, meeting them at trading posts set up in northern Mexico. The Lipans, Jicarillas, and Mescaleros willingly swapped buffalo hides for grain and trinkets. The Apaches also picked up other items from the Spanish. One such item was cattle, which the Apaches found tasty and nutritious. Another was firearms, Spanish *harquebuses*, or muskets. These large guns lacked the range of the bow and arrow and took much longer to load, but Apache warriors used them effectively to frighten people during raids.

Of much greater value were horses. They afforded Apache warriors tremendous mobility and doubled as pack animals when a group moved camp. Horses also increased Apache contact with other tribes and expanded their opportunities for trade. What the Apaches liked most about horses was their meat. It became a main source of sustenance for them.

The Spanish were interested in obtaining goods that were not up for barter—Apache slaves—and hunted them ruthlessly. In the process, they probably introduced the gruesome practice of scalping, quickly adopted by the Apaches, who fought back at every turn. By 1660, a constant state of guerrilla warfare existed between the two peoples. Spanish horsemen terrorized Apache camps, and the Apaches frequently set upon the settlers, seizing human captives, horses, cattle, and guns.

In approximately 1688, the Apaches mounted numerous raids on Sonora, a northern Mexican state bordering Arizona. The Spaniards fought back but were confused by the Apaches, whose nomadic habits made them difficult to pin down in pitched battles. The mobility of the Apaches enabled them to dictate the time and place of a contest, and the Spaniards worried that they might lose their foothold in northern Mexico. Vicious fighting occurred in the eighteenth century. Some historians estimate that between 1748 and 1770, the Apaches killed four thousand Spanish settlers and stole or destroyed millions of dollars worth of property.

In 1786, Bernardo de Gálvez, a skilled Indian fighter, became viceroy of Mexico and wrote a treatise, *Instructions for the Governing of the Interior Provinces of New Spain*. Gálvez's treatise drew on some of the warlike policies established by his predecessors, but not all its measures were overtly hostile. For instance, Gálvez urged local colonial authorities to give the Indians gifts, food, and alcohol. He explained that charity would make the Indians dependent on the Spanish, especially when they emptied their flasks. "The supplying of drink to the Indians," Gálvez wrote, "will be a means of gaining their goodwill, discovering their secrets, calming them so they will think less of conceiving and executing their hostilities, and creating for them a new necessity which will oblige them to recognize their dependence upon us more directly." Gálvez also advised that Indians be given faulty muskets so that they would have to rely on the Spanish to repair them.

It is impossible to know how this approach would have fared over time because Gálvez died within months of taking

Bernardo de Gálvez, who led numerous military expeditions against the Apaches in the northern Mexico provinces of Sonora and Nueva Vizcaya during the early 1770s, espoused a policy of providing gifts to Natives so that they would become dependent on Spanish charity and thus let down their guard. Unfortunately, Gálvez, who became New Spain's viceroy in 1785, died the following year and he could never implement his *Instructions for the Governing of the Interior Provinces of New Spain*.

office. He was replaced by Manuel Antonio Flores, who advocated outright extermination of the Indians and increased the number of troops sent into their territory. The Apaches, defeated in battle, retreated north to Tucson and Tubac (in Arizona). Today the ruins of Tubac's Spanish *presidio*, or fort, still stand, forty miles south of Tucson on the Santa Cruz River, just north of the Mexican border.

Some Apaches fled, but others resumed raiding, angered by the change in the Spanish Indian policy after Flores succeeded Gálvez. In 1789 Flores resigned, citing ill health, and yet another viceroy, Conde de Revillagigedo, took over. His policy reverted to the peaceful means promoted by Gálvez. He sought to establish alliances with the Apaches and provided them with supplies. It seemed peace had come to *Gran Apacheria* (roughly translated, Great Apache land)—but it proved short lived.

As the nineteenth century began, the Spanish government abandoned its plan of peaceful coexistence. Furnishing the Apaches with clothing, food, and liquor drained community funds. Taxes were introduced, but Spanish colonists objected to paying them. Thus, the Apaches saw their supplies dwindle. Those bands camped near the colonists began to drift away, joining forces with those who had never yielded to the Spaniards' offer of friendship. Soon butchery resumed—on both sides. The Spanish continued to take a peaceful approach to the Apaches on only one front: religion. From the outset of their colonial adventures in the New World, the Spaniards had tried to wean Native peoples away from their own religion and toward Roman Catholicism. Church missionaries, such as Friar Marcos, traveled with conquistadores. As the conquerors subdued Indians by force, holy men tried to guide them peaceably into the Christian faith by "educating" them at missionary churches staffed by clergy. Sometimes missionaries were the first white men ever glimpsed by Indians. This was so especially in the southeastern areas of North America, in present-day Florida and Georgia, where by the early 1600s there may have been forty different missions supervising the lives of twenty thousand Indians, all of whom converted to Christianity.

To these religious emissaries, the Apache religion—their gods, legends, and rituals—seemed crude and barbaric. The Apaches, in turn, viewed Christianity as alien. Christians worshiped inside buildings and fixed their attention on a raised altar that depicted the suffering body of Christ. The Apaches conducted their ceremonies outdoors and lifted their gaze toward the limitless vault of the sky.

Nonetheless, many Apaches were converted from their own religion to Roman Catholicism, though not always with the results hoped for by missionaries. In fact, one convert became a scourge to the very people who took him under their wing. His name was Juan José, and he lived in the early nineteenth century. Juan José was born a Mimbres Apache of the Eastern Chiricahua band. At an early age, he was packed off by Spanish authorities to a mission school, one of the numerous places where Roman Catholicism was taught to Indian children. Juan José had an aptitude for learning and was encouraged by his teachers to study for the priesthood. He heeded their advice and dedicated himself to Christianity—until 1835, when he discovered that his father had been murdered by Mexicans.

Juan José abruptly quit the mission and returned to his band, anxious for revenge. He rose to a high position and led a group of warriors who mounted vicious attacks on Mexican settlements. Because Juan José had been exposed to the ways of the settlers, he knew how best to weaken them. He robbed their mail and captured messengers, forcing them to divulge crucial information.

Even as he wreaked havoc among the colonists, Juan José stayed on friendly terms with a trader in Sonora, Mexico—an American named James Johnson, who bought Juan José's stolen goods. Their relationship was on solid footing when the Apaches intercepted a letter to Johnson sent by the Mexican government, which offered the trader a handsome reward for Juan José's scalp. Juan José confronted Johnson with this evidence, but the American convinced him of his loyalty and then accepted an invitation to the Apaches' camp. Johnson arrived laden with gifts. He heaped them in a pile that contained a hidden fuse. As the Apaches crowded around, Johnson secretly tossed a match, igniting a howitzer (a small cannon). It spat out lead projectiles that killed many Apaches and wounded others, including Juan José, who struggled with one of Johnson's American companions. Johnson then shot José in the back, killing him and betraying their friendship.

The Apaches were embittered by other, similar episodes. One of them occurred in the summer of 1850. At that time many Warm Springs Apaches—of the Eastern Chiricahua band—camped along the San Miguel River near Ramos, about eighty miles south of Columbus, New Mexico. The band traded in town during the day, and at night they sang, danced, and gambled in their camp.

One day local Mexicans invited the Apaches into Ramos to join them in drinking *mescal*, a type of liquor distilled from spiny leaves of maguey plants. The Mexicans furnished an unlimited supply of the alcohol free of charge, and many of the Indians became intoxicated. They returned to the camp and fell into a drunken sleep. Then, before dawn, the Mexican villagers crept into the Apache camp and began killing the sleeping Indians. Jason Betzinger and W.S. Nye describe the scene in *I Fought with Geronimo*: "There were curses in Spanish, thuds, grunts, a few screams, and the whimpering of a child. Here and there a rustle told where some more alert Indian managed to steal away in the semi-darkness. But there were few such. In a short time most of the Indians were lying in their blood, dead or dying."

Throughout this period, Spanish-Mexican officials formally kept up peaceful relations with the Apaches. Viceroys instituted different strategies, some favoring war, others peace, while in reality confusion reigned. The State of Sonora put a bounty on the head of all Apache men, women, and children. It was difficult, however, to distinguish an Apache scalp from any other. John Terrell writes in *Apache Chronicle* that "on several occasions bounty hunters wiped out Mexican villages, scalped their victims, young and old, male and female, and delivered

After Mexico gained its independence from Spain in 1821, the Apaches, who originally acquired guns from the Spanish in the 1700s, began to increase their raids into Mexico. Despite signing peace treaties with the Mexican government in return for an annual supply of gun powder and corn, the Apaches' raiding into Mexico reached a highpoint during the mid-1860s, when tens of thousands of dollars worth of livestock was taken from bordering provinces in Mexico.

the scalps to the authorities for payment with the claim that they had been taken from Apaches."

One reason the situation became so violent was that Mexico was trying to consolidate its power as part of its struggle for independence from Spain. As early as 1810, Mexican colonials led by Hidalgo y Costilla, a priest, had rebelled against the mother country. During the next decade, Mexican insurrectionists battled troops loyal to Spain, and in 1821, Spain accepted Mexico's independence as a European-style monarchy. Two years later, a republic was set up, but the government was run by self-serving individuals who vied for power and wealth. Mexico suffered through a succession of leaders, none able to cure its economic and social ills.

The problems intensified in 1846, when Mexico went to war with the United States over Texas—which at the time belonged to Mexico—whose citizens wanted to make the future state an independent republic. The fighting lasted two years and ended with Mexico's surrender to the United States in 1848. The *Treaty of Guadalupe Hidalgo* granted independence to Texas and ceded to the United States a vast territory that included the northern parts of New Mexico and Arizona. Five years later, the southern parts of these states went to the United States as part of the *Gadsden Purchase*, a $10 million sale that enabled the U.S. government to construct a southern railroad through areas inhabited by Indians.

The 1848 treaty included a provision that had important consequences for the Apaches. The United States agreed to prevent Indians residing in its newly acquired lands from going south to raid settlements in Mexico. If such raids occurred, the United States agreed to punish those responsible and to stop its own citizens from purchasing goods or livestock brought back over the border. The Americans also agreed to compensate Mexicans for any losses they sustained. This provision pitted the United States against the Apaches, for whom raiding had become habit. A new enemy of the Indian had emerged.

5

The Americans

At the time Texas was pushing for liberation from Mexico, it had a large population of English-speaking Americans. By 1834, twenty thousand settlers had moved to the settlement of Austin and outnumbered Mexicans in the region four to one. After the United States won the Mexican War, a general westward expansion began as people living in the established states on the eastern seaboard yearned for land and space.

In 1848, gold was discovered in California. Over the next two years, thousands of American and European prospectors streamed across the continent in search of the precious ore. In the 1850s, the pioneer spirit took hold. Railroads enabled farmers in the Midwest—Illinois, Iowa, Minnesota, and neighboring states—to transport goods back east. The 1860s and '70s saw an influx of farmers from Germany and Scandinavia who trekked to western territories that, as a result of the 1862 Homestead Act, offered 160 acres practically free to anyone willing to cultivate them.

By the mid-nineteenth century, more than 200,000 Indians inhabited the Great Plains and the Rocky Mountains. During this time, they faced the arrival of American miners, railroads, and cattlemen, all assisted by the U.S. government, which had declared a policy of Manifest Destiny meant to expand the nation's borders to California and the Pacific Ocean. The Indians, separated into distinct nations that were subdivided further into tribes, bands, and local groups, struggled to hold back the tide.

The Apaches proved especially fierce in the defense of their land and way of life. They came into conflict with the United States soon after it acquired Texas (which was granted statehood in 1845) and the vast territory ceded by Mexico. Among a total population of about one hundred thousand, there were sixty thousand Mexicans. The rest were Indians, six thousand to eight thousand of them Apaches. This tiny number had little chance of fending off the U.S. Army, which governed the area.

At first the Apaches fought the troops, but then, in 1850, leaders of the Mescaleros in New Mexico's Sierra Blancas informed the U.S. military that they would exchange all their captives and stolen property and sign a *treaty*. The Mescalero chiefs called a meeting with the Jicarillas and Comanches. The various bands stopped raiding and awaited developments. The Americans, who had only 1,300 soldiers, agreed to end hostilities. In 1851, James S. Calhoun—governor of New Mexico Territory and its superintendent of Indian Affairs—signed a treaty with the Jicarillas and with two Mescalero leaders, Lobo and Josécito. An enlightened man, Calhoun sought to extend the pact. He planned to visit another Apache band, the Eastern Chiricahuas, who were camped at Santa Rita.

Calhoun's good intentions met with resistance from the U.S. Army. A change of command put a new officer in charge

Apaches were steadfast in protecting their territory from white settlers who attempted to move onto their land after the Mexican War ended in 1848. As part of the terms of the Treaty of Guadalupe Hidalgo, Mexico ceded most of what is today the American Southwest to the United States. Eventually the Apaches were forced to settle on one of five reservations that the U.S. government established for them during the early 1870s. Shown here are three White Mountain Apaches who were confined to Fort Apache Indian Reservation in east-central Arizona.

of the Ninth Military Department, which supervised affairs in New Mexico. He was Edwin Vose Sumner, who in 1851 arrived in New Mexico and completely altered the strategy there. He removed troops from the towns where they had been posted and stationed them at forts situated in key places. The soldiers were ordered to build these posts themselves, and many sprang up, including Fort Webster, erected in Apache territory.

At the same time that Sumner initiated this new strategy, he was expected to cooperate with Calhoun, who still occupied the post of governor and superintendent. Sumner took his first responsibility—to quell any Indian threat—more seriously than his second. He halted Calhoun's attempt to make peace with the Warm Springs Apaches of the Eastern Chiricahua band.

The Warm Springs Apaches were known in their own language as the *Tcihe-ende*, or "Red-paint People," because of the color of their war paint, a broad clay stripe across the face. Their leader, Mangas Coloradas (Spanish for Red Sleeves), the successor to Juan José, was the most imposing Apache chief of his time. A physical giant who was also intelligent and shrewd, he behaved in the classic manner of the Apache leader. So respected was he that his following reached beyond his own band.

Mangas had little respect for whites, or *pindah-lickoyee* (white-eyed enemies), and his contempt for them grew when prospectors working the mines at Santa Rita killed Apaches without provocation and without being punished by the U.S. government. Yet Mangas dealt with the whites on their terms. Instead of avenging the murder of his people, he insisted only that those responsible be tried for the crime. Mangas changed his approach, however, when a new gold-mining site was built at a nearby spot, Piños Altos. The chief visited the miners and asked them to leave, recommending that they move south of the border to Sonora, which had richer deposits of ore. Suspecting a ruse, the miners tied the chief to a post, whipped him mercilessly, and then taunted him as he staggered away.

Mangas got his revenge. In February 1852, he began a rampage that the Americans could not stop. The Apaches raided mail carriages and murdered those aboard, plundered a federal wagon train (only the drivers escaped), and killed soldiers sent to capture them. U.S. troops did not catch Mangas until 1863, when he was in his sixties, and then only by deception. A group of forty prospectors traveling through Apache territory decided to kidnap Mangas in order to forestall conflict with his band. They persuaded a military unit to back them and then asked Mangas to appear at their camp to discuss terms for peace. Mangas arrived and was whisked away to a military camp. He was interrogated, tortured, and shot. The soldiers then scalped him and sent his skull to a phrenologist (a person who analyzes one's character by studying the shape of the subject's skull; phrenology is a pseudoscience that was popular in Europe and the United States in the nineteenth century).

Thievery, murder, and massacre—conducted by both Americans and Apaches—plunged the Southwest into another violent phase. Sometimes safety could be found only in the old forts of Tucson and Tubac. In 1850, the Apaches attacked Tucson. According to *Victorio and the Mimbres Apaches*, by historian Dan Thrapp, "Anything went, provided one could seize the advantage. Even such servants of mercy as physicians were not above falling into line. One doctor, called upon to treat an Apache whose leg had been punctured by a bullet, unnecessarily amputated the limb at the hip . . . since he believed him to be . . . [a frequent] raider."

Captain John Bourke described the effects of an Apache attack on a wagon train:

> It was a ghastly sight . . . There were the hot embers of the new wagons, the scattered fragments of broken boxes, barrels and packages of all sorts, broken rifles, torn and burned clothing. There lay all that was mortal of poor [pioneer Newton] Israel, stripped of clothing, a small piece cut from the crown of the head, but thrown back upon the corpse— the Apache do not care much for scalping—his heart cut out, but also thrown back near the corpse, which had been dragged to the fire of the burning wagons and had been

partly consumed; a lance wound in the back, one or two arrow wounds . . . a severe contusion under the left eye, where he had been hit, perhaps with the stock of a rifle or carbine, and the death wound from ear to ear.

Another violent incident occurred in the winter of 1863–64 and involved the Pinal and Coyotero bands, both subdivisions of the Western Apaches. Indians had stolen livestock from settlers living near Peeple Valley in Yavapai County, about twenty miles southwest of Prescott, Arizona. In January 1864, King Woolsey, an aide to the territorial governor of Arizona—it was not yet a state—led a group of settlers against the raiders. His terse report of the conflict, quoted by Frank Lockwood in *Apache Indians*, published in 1938, described the incident in this way: "On January 24, 1864, a party of thirty Americans and fourteen Maricopa and Pima Indians . . . attacked a band of Gila Apaches and killed nineteen of them and wounded others. Mr. Cyrus Lennon Woolsey's party was killed by a wounded Indian."

In truth, the battle was more complicated, at least according to stories circulated by Arizona pioneers who stated that the Apaches trapped Woolsey and his party in the Tonto Basin, south of Payson in Gila County. The Apaches held the high ground above the pioneers, who called a truce. Through an interpreter, Woolsey called a council with about thirty of the Indian warriors. Before going off to meet them, he instructed a rear guard of some two hundred men to open fire when he touched his hat. Woolsey then set off with three other men, each carrying a concealed revolver. They met with the Apache warriors, who had hidden weapons of their own—knives. After the meeting began, a young Apache boy arrived with the news that their leader wanted his warriors to return in order to help kill the whites and their Indian allies. At this point, Woolsey touched his hat and his men loosed their fire.

Yet another grim episode, known as the Camp Grant Massacre, occurred on April 30, 1871. The preceding February,

150 Aravaipas, another Western Apache band, sought refuge at Camp Grant, located about sixty miles northeast of Tucson. These Apaches feared U.S. troops and had taken to living in the mountains, where freezing temperatures and a poor food supply had caused many in the group to die. They hoped to return to their former home near Aravaipa Creek, where they could plant crops and live more comfortably. This home happened to be in the vicinity of Camp Grant, and the Apaches appeared there one day and asked for permission to live nearby, under the protection of the U.S. troops.

The garrison's ranking officer, Lieutenant Royal Emerson Whitman, invited the Apaches to stay on the premises while he awaited approval from his superiors in California. Whitman provided the Apaches with rations and let them gather food in the surrounding area. He also employed them as hay gatherers for the garrison's horses, paying them a penny per pound. Soon the number of Apaches grew to five hundred as word spread among groups that Lieutenant Whitman could be counted on for assistance and protection. In April, a new commander, Captain Frank Stanwood, arrived at the fort. Whitman explained the unusual arrangement, and Stanwood approved it. Two weeks later, word finally came from California, but it was useless: Whitman's letter did not conform exactly to U.S. Army regulations, so the general had declined to answer it, a convenient way to ignore the issue.

Nonetheless, the arrangement continued. Later in April, Captain Stanwood left camp on a long scouting mission, taking most of the troops with him. Whitman stayed behind with about fifty soldiers. Stanwood had not yet returned on April 30, when a messenger appeared at Camp Grant and informed him that a civilian posse from Tucson, which had suffered repeated Apache raids, was riding toward Camp Grant. Whitman immediately sent interpreters to warn the Indians and direct them to shelter inside the fort.

It was too late. A mob of 148 civilians—6 whites, 48

Mexicans, and 94 Papago Indians (another southwestern people), with ammunition and provisions furnished by the adjutant general of Arizona Territory—set upon the sleeping Apaches. The Indians had no weapons. Worse yet, the men in the camp had gone hunting in the mountains, leaving the women and children defenseless. One hundred people were shot or clubbed to death. Twenty-nine children survived, and the vigilantes took them as captives. Two escaped; five ended up in the hands of Arizona citizens, who turned them over to the U.S. government; the remaining twenty-two were sold into slavery in Mexico. American newspapers gloried in the bloodshed. The *Denver News* crowed: "We give this act of the citizens of Arizona most hearty and unqualified endorsement. We congratulate them on the fact that permanent peace arrangements have been made with so many, and we regret that the number was not double."

The president of the United States, Ulysses S. Grant (1869–77), was horrified by the incident and demanded that the vigilantes be tried. Charges were brought against 104 people, and the jury deliberated for 20 minutes before finding them all innocent.

Desolation, destruction, and death seemed the bywords of the new territories. An article written in 1910 in Texas' *El Paso Morning Times* summarized the feeling of most Americans: "The only means of persuasion at the time with an Apache was by means of a Winchester with a cool head and a clear eye at the other end."

As that comment indicates, Texas had a history of treating the Apaches badly. In 1855, two small reservations were set aside in the northern area of the state for its population of Mescaleros, and there was talk of granting the band more land. Yet in 1859, before any reservation could be established, vigilantes raided the already existing reserves, and concerned officials quickly sent Indians to protected territory in Oklahoma. After the demise of the Texas reservations, Texans considered the remaining Mescaleros fair game. When Major Robert Neighbors, the U.S. superintendent of Indian Affairs for Texas, tried to protect the band and its property, he was assassinated.

New Mexico proved equally hostile to the Mescaleros living there. The territory grew in population as new lands were opened by the U.S. government after the discovery of gold in California in 1848 and in nearby Colorado in 1859, and following the Mexican War and the Gadsden Purchase. Prospectors poured into the area, and settlers occupied land that had traditionally belonged to the Mescaleros. These newcomers also killed buffalo and other game prized by the Apaches. Worse, they did it for sport rather than for sustenance.

The Mescaleros attacked the settlers, hoping to drive them off the land. The U.S. military responded in kind. Forts arose throughout the Mescalero area and conflict raged on. During the Civil War (1861–65), some Union troops were stationed in the Southwest. One of their commanders, General James H. Carleton, who had fought the Jicarillas in 1854, decided to clear up the problem. In 1862, he ordered some of his men to build a post in east-central New Mexico—Fort Sumner—near a place called Bosque Redondo (Spanish for Round Grove) on the Pecos River, where some cottonwoods grew. There, on an area of about forty square miles, Carleton intended to create a reservation. All the local Indians were ordered to appear there. A total of nine thousand Navajos and five hundred Mescaleros complied in order to escape murder at the hands of Carleton's forces.

The area could not support so large a population, however, and by 1864 the Mescaleros and Navajos had begun squabbling. Most of the Mescaleros escaped and made their way back to their traditional lands. In 1866, U.S. Army authorities relieved Carleton of his command, and the U.S. government concluded that the Bosque was unsuitable for a reservation.

In 1872, the federal government attempted to establish a separate reservation for the Mescaleros. The next year, an executive order issued by President Grant established reservations on the eastern slopes of the White and Sacramento mountains, located in south-central New Mexico, east of the Rio Grande. Any Mescaleros found outside these designated areas would be treated as hostile by the military. In 1880, the U.S. government ordered the band to Fort Stanton, also in south-central New Mexico. When they arrived, they were stripped of their weapons and horses. Fourteen Mescaleros resisted. The soldiers killed them. Others fled. Those who submitted to the troops were held in a corral filled with manure. Some Apaches grew ill, and the authorities were compelled to release them with the stipulation that they remain near the fort. Later that year they moved into a reservation.

The troubles between the Jicarillas and the United States began after the United States acquired New Mexico. In October 1849, Jicarilla warriors joined those from another Indian nation, the *Ute*, in an attack on U.S. troops at the Cimarron River cutoff of the *Santa Fe Trail*. The next month they struck the trail again, raiding an eastbound mail party. U.S. forces retaliated, and a pattern began that lasted through the year. In 1850, the U.S. Army built forts in Jicarilla territory.

The next year, the band signed a treaty with the U.S. government. They agreed to stop raiding settlements, to return what they had stolen, to live by farming, and to accept confinement within a reservation. In return the U.S. government offered them financial aid. The treaty failed, however, to win approval from the U.S. Congress, and the Jicarillas received no assistance from the federal government. They nevertheless abided by the unratified agreement and staged only a few raids.

In 1852, William Lane, the territorial governor, began settling the band on land west of the Rio Grande on the Rio Puerco. He was acting on his own—the federal government had not authorized such a reservation. One Jicarilla band cleared more than a hundred acres and planted crops, eliminating their need to raid. Lane seemed to have hit upon the ideal solution for lessening hostilities, but he was ordered to suspend his program by the federal government in Washington, D.C.

As a result, the Jicarillas resumed raiding in order to feed themselves. In 1854, the acting governor of New Mexico declared war on the band. He sent an army after them, and it pursued the Jicarillas throughout northern New Mexico and southern Colorado. Eventually, both sides agreed to negotiate and signed another peace treaty in September 1855. Again, approval failed to come from Congress, which remained skeptical. The Jicarillas continued to live in the area and supported themselves by hunting, farming, and gathering.

From 1855 to 1887, the U.S. government mulled over various plans for coming to terms with the Jicarillas, who by 1873 were the only tribe in New Mexico not living on a reservation. A favored, yet unsuccessful, solution was to settle the Jicarillas on reservations alongside other Indians. In 1873, the parties signed yet a third treaty. It granted the band a reservation in northwestern New Mexico. White settlers demanded this land, however, and in 1876 the territorial government refused to abide by the treaty's provisions.

Four years later, the U.S. government established another reservation for the Jicarillas in north-central New Mexico. Again, the program failed, and the band was sent to the Mescalero Reservation. In 1887, the U.S. government reestablished the reservation opened in 1880, and the Jicarillas finally came into land of their own.

The Western Apaches lived in east-central Arizona. After the United States acquired that territory as part of the Gadsden Purchase, conflicts arose. As was the case with the other Apaches, settlers and miners encroached on their land. Hostilities erupted and lasted some forty years. In 1864, the United States established Camp Goodwin on the Gila River in White Mountain Apache territory. The fort isolated the White Mountain and Cibecue Apaches. These Western bands—mindful of the fate that befell other Apaches—quickly made peace with the U.S. government. They continued to raid Mexican villages, however.

By the late nineteenth century, it was clear to the Apaches that the U.S. government intended to pin them on the margins of the growing republic. Following the Camp Grant Massacre, the U.S. government initiated a new peace policy designed to gather all the Apaches on reservations. The plan called for each of the Apache bands to be given its own land, where they could live unmolested by white miners and settlers and where they could be taught to farm, so that raiding would no longer be necessary.

In 1871–72, the federal government established four Apache reservations in Arizona. The Cibecues and the northern bands of the White Mountain Apaches were given the area around Fort Apache, in east-central Arizona. Camp Verde, northeast of Phoenix, Arizona, went to the Northern and Southern Tontos and some of the Yavapais. The San Carlos Apaches and the Southern White Mountain groups moved to San Carlos, in southeastern Arizona, and the Chiricahuas were granted a reservation in Cochise County, in southeastern Arizona.

At first it seemed this policy might eliminate warfare between the Apaches and the United States. In 1872, General George Crook, a longtime Indian fighter celebrated for his conquest of the Paiute Nation, was placed in command of the Arizona Department, following the Camp Grant Massacre. Crook sympathized with the Apache plight and generally treated them fairly. He knew that they fought because they had to. "The American Indian commands respect," he once remarked, "only as long as he inspires terror with his rifle."

Crook's appointed task, however, was to subdue the Apaches, and he set about doing this with all the fervor of a dedicated military man. He had some novel ideas about how best to fight the Apaches. He abandoned wagon trains for pack mules that could negotiate the mountainous terrain where the Apaches liked to conduct warfare. Crook thought

Geronimo, pictured here in 1887, helped carry on the Chiricahua Apaches' war with the United States after Cochise's death in 1874. When the Apaches finally surrendered in 1886—the last major Native group to do so—Geronimo and his band were first sent to Florida, then Alabama, and finally to the Fort Sill Reservation in Oklahoma.

that U.S. soldiers who were not familiar with the rigors of the desert were no match for Apache warriors, with their remarkable stamina and durability. Thus, he favored winning over friendly Apaches to act as scouts and fighters in his army. Crook's approach met with disapproval from Americans who balked at the prospect of fighting side by side with Indians.

As Apache raids continued, Crook began a campaign to scoop up all the Apaches not settled on reservations. In 1872, he moved against the Tonto band and defeated them in a few months. Then, in 1874, U.S. policy shifted once more, this time toward "concentration." This policy dictated that three Apache bands—the Western, Chiricahua, and Yavapai—be placed on one reservation, San Carlos, where they could be managed more easily. In 1875, the U.S. government began gathering the

Geronimo, The Last Warrior

Geronimo was born in the early 1820s in the area that is now southwestern Arizona. Not until he was nearly eighty years old did the short and muscular warrior surrender to U.S. Army forces at Skeleton Canyon, on the border of New Mexico and Mexico, approximately one hundred miles from his birthplace. Geronimo was the last Apache leader to resist capture by U.S. Army forces. In fact, he never was captured but voluntarily led his rebel Chiricahua band to surrender in 1886 to end the era of the Apache wars in the American Southwest.

Geronimo had submitted to captivity on an Arizona reservation twice before but each time changed his mind and escaped to Mexico, where he hid with other Indians in the Sierra Madre. Along the way, Geronimo raided Mexican and American villages, stole horses and cattle, and murdered innocent people. He was accused of even more violence and savagery by U.S. Army officials and the American public. Eventually, Geronimo came to symbolize Indian ferocity. After his final surrender, he was known as "the Apache terror."

One army aide, Britton Davis, who was in charge of leading the Indian scouts who searched for Geronimo's hideouts, described the warrior as "a thoroughly vicious . . . and treacherous man. His only redeeming traits were courage and determinism. His word, no matter how earnestly pledged, was worthless." Geronimo, however, claimed otherwise. "I never do wrong without a cause," he declared. "Several times I have asked for peace, but trouble has come from the agents and interpreters."

Apaches. It was a flawed idea. Forcing different bands to live together caused hostility and suspicion among them. Factions arose. Some groups wanted war, others peace, still others to escape. Many did flee, and General Crook was ordered to track them down, especially those Chiricahuas who had broken away and mounted several raids.

Perhaps the most tenacious of all the Apache bands was the Chiricahuas, who launched a twenty-five-year war against the

Despite his skillful leadership in battle, Geronimo never held the post of war chief. He was instead a *di-yin*, or shaman, who gained others' respect and awe by using powers he believed were granted to him by supernatural spirits. In wartime, Geronimo relied on his clairvoyance and called on spirits to help him discover enemy camps, pray for victory, and make war charms that brought protection and good luck. One follower credited Geronimo with having once stopped the sun and extended night for two hours so that the war party could approach the enemy in the dark.

In 1895, after Geronimo's final surrender and relocation to Fort Sill, Oklahoma, he no longer summoned his supernatural powers. He turned instead to other survival instincts that allowed him to prosper in captivity even as many of his compatriots struggled and died. Gifted with a keen business sense, Geronimo sold autographs, photographs, and buttons from his coat to tourists. Painters paid him to sit for portraits, and exhibitors paid him to appear in Indian shows. In 1905, he received $171 to ride in costume on horseback in President Theodore Roosevelt's inaugural parade as proof of the U.S. government's intention to "civilize" Indians. In the same year, Geronimo began dictating his own version of his transformation from free Apache to prisoner of war. S.M. Barrett, a school superintendent, wrote down the account, which was published in 1907 as *Geronimo's Story of His Life*.

In 1909, at about the age of eighty, Geronimo got drunk one night at Fort Sill. He fell off of his horse and into a creek, where he lay until the next morning. He did not drown, but he developed pneumonia and soon died.

United States in northern Mexico, Arizona, and New Mexico. The battle began in October 1860, when Apaches from an unidentified band raided a ranch owned by the Wards, home-steaders near Tubac, Arizona. The band spirited away livestock and the Wards' 12-year-old son, Felix. His father, John Ward, followed the raiders' trail and became convinced they were Chiricahuas led by the renowned warrior Cochise. Ward reported his beliefs to the commanding officer at Fort Buchanan, and in January 1860 approximately fifty soldiers were sent to Apache Pass in southeastern Arizona. Their newly commissioned second lieutenant, George Bascom, was ordered to recover the boy and the cattle, by force if necessary.

After reaching the pass, Bascom's company camped in Siphon Canyon, about a mile from Fort Bowie near a stage-coach station. Cochise appeared with an escort of warriors, one carrying a white flag. Bascom and Cochise exchanged polite greetings. Then the Apaches entered Bascom's tent. Bascom accused Cochise of stealing the livestock and kidnapping the boy. Cochise denied having any knowledge of the incident and offered to help obtain information and to recover the boy. Bascom then called Cochise a liar and told him that he and his warriors would be imprisoned if Felix Ward and the stolen cat-tle were not returned.

The lieutenant had anticipated trouble with Cochise and had previously ordered soldiers to surround the tent. They now closed in. Cochise suddenly pulled out his knife and slit open the wall to Bascom's tent. He climbed through it and escaped the camp, eluding gunfire. His six warriors remained in Bascom's custody, however. The next day Cochise returned to the stagecoach station with a chief of the Coyotero band and five hundred warriors. Cochise took the stationmaster captive and killed two other employees who tried to escape.

That night Cochise attacked the eastbound Overland Mail Coach and a small wagon train. He brutally killed all the team-sters—or drivers—except three, whom he took captive.

Occasional fighting continued during the next several days. Cochise held the upper hand over Bascom and his small company. Then two columns of U.S. soldiers arrived at Apache Pass, and the Chiricahuas retreated into the surrounding hills. On February 18, the combined U.S. military forces marched out of the pass. The troops observed a flock of buzzards circling overhead. Officers sent advance scouts to investigate. They discovered the corpses of Cochise's captives.

The senior U.S. officer, Colonel Bernard John Dowling Irwin, who had arrived at the head of one of the relief columns, ordered the execution of the Apaches still in his custody. Three of them were related by blood to Cochise. Within 60 days, the Chiricahuas killed 150 white people, and for years no traveler found safety along the Overland Trail.

Cochise had not been lying to Bascom. It was a band of Pinal, Western Apaches, who had raided the Ward ranch. Had Bascom been more experienced he would not have doubted the chief's word. Seasoned soldiers and U.S. government officials had learned to trust Cochise and to hold him in high regard. And indeed he was one of the premier Indian leaders of his era. The son-in-law of Mangas Coloradas, Cochise had won a loyal following by the time of the Chiricahua Wars. He was then in his late thirties, an average-sized man who excelled in combat as a strategist and fighter. He was also a skilled raider who provided amply for his band and could be counted on for guidance and sympathy.

In 1872, Cochise agreed to a peace treaty that gave the Chiricahuas a reservation on their homeland in southeastern Arizona. Two years later, Cochise died. In 1875, the *Bureau of Indian Affairs* (BIA) reported that raids in the area had ceased. The bureau's policy of concentration shattered this long-awaited calm. The Chiricahuas objected to being removed from their homeland to the San Carlos Agency, a reservation in south-central Arizona. The band disliked both the land and the agency. As one Apache told Eve Ball, author of *In the Days of*

Shortly after they surrendered to U.S. troops in September 1886, Geronimo and his band of Chiricahua Apaches were transported to Florida, where they were exiled as prisoners of war. Shown here is Geronimo's band preparing to be transported to San Antonio's Fort Sam Houston, on the first leg of their trip to Florida.

Victorio: "Take stones and ashes and thorns, with some scorpions and rattlesnakes thrown in, dump the outfit on stones, heat the stones red hot, set the United States Army after the Apaches, and you have San Carlos." The Chiricahuas also regarded the other Apaches at San Carlos with hostility and suspicion. Even so, in 1876 the U.S. government abolished the Chiricahua Reservation and moved 322 people—mainly women, children, and old men—to the new place. The remainder fled to the Warm Springs Reservation, to the mountains, or to Mexico.

Two years later, a band led by Geronimo, raided American settlements in southern Arizona and New Mexico. He was captured quickly and sent to San Carlos, but he eventually escaped.

That year the U.S. government also subjected the Warm Springs band to the concentration policy, but only 450 out of a total population of 2,000 could be rounded up for removal. The rest formed raiding groups led by Chief Victorio. A tragic and unbreakable cycle of Apache behavior had emerged—one of surrender, escape, and raid, repeated until the band had exhausted its numbers and strength.

In October 1880, Mexicans destroyed Victorio's raiding band at Tres Castillos in northern Mexico. Of the Warm Springs Apaches, only the leader Naña and his followers remained on the loose. At long last, on September 4, 1886, Geronimo finally surrendered. Peace had come to Gran Apacheria. The U.S. government decided to rid itself of the Chiricahua problem by classifying all its living members as prisoners of war and exiling them, first to Florida, then to Alabama, and finally to Oklahoma. Geronimo went into exile, along with his followers and 382 others, including some of the U.S. Army's own Apache scouts. Most of the band's graves are located at Fort Sill, Oklahoma.

6

Reservation Life

By 1890, all the Apache bands had submitted to the U.S. government's reservation policy, which recognized them as distinct subgroups functioning outside the mainstream of American society. The Apaches were not entirely free of the U.S. government, however. The BIA vowed to turn reservations into "schools for civilization." By this time, the total American-Indian population had been reduced to about 300,000, less than one-third of what it had been when Columbus first landed in the New World.

Although reservations were meant to recognize the separateness of America's Indian population, they served mainly to transfer control over Indian life from the U.S. Army to the BIA, which supervised law enforcement, education, health, and land development. In 1878, the BIA set up a police force that had almost unlimited power to prosecute and punish Indians. Within six years, the U.S. Indian Police—all white men—operated in forty-eight of the sixty reservations.

By 1890, all Apache bands had been placed on reservations by the U.S. government. Shown here is a group of Apache boys on the Mescalero Apache Reservation in south-central New Mexico.

The key white figure on each reservation was the agent, a U.S. government official who assumed the task of "civilizing" Indians. In general that meant converting Indians to Christianity and instructing them in farming. Tilling the soil brought unwelcome changes to age-old Indian cultures. Jacob Dunn voiced a commonly held view when he asserted in *Massacres of the Mountains*, published in 1886, that the typical Apache warrior could not "feel that fighting is the only work that a man ought to do, and then take kindly to ploughing. His spirit must be broken in some way, or his nature changed, before he will submit to it. The right or wrong of breaking his spirit is another question; the fact remains that he must be born again in civilization."

"Born again" was another phrase, like "schools for civilization," that sounded loftier than its actual purpose proved. For in the early years of the reservations, the true aim of the U.S. government was the systematic destruction of the Apache way of life, which was to be replaced with, in the ringing tones of one noted Indian agent, Dr. Michael Steck, a "laudable desire to accumulate and retain property." Thus, agents discouraged traditional Apache ceremonies, such as the healing rituals, that involved giving away material goods. The Indian Police functioned, on the whole, as a means to strip power away from traditional group and band leaders. When the Apaches resisted, agents often threatened to reduce their food rations. In fact, the threat of starvation became the preferred method of "civilizing" Indians. After a century of effort, the U.S. government's twin project—guiding the Apaches toward both Christianity and farming—has met with mixed success. Many have become Christians, yet shamans still are sought out as healers. All Apaches learn English but most prefer to use their own language. Ceremonies, such as the girls' puberty rite, are still practiced by many Apaches.

Gradually, the U.S. government has come to recognize that Indians are proud of their heritage and want to preserve it—without being denied the opportunities given other Americans. In March 1968, President Lyndon B. Johnson (1963–69) sent a message on Indian affairs to Congress. He proposed to "erase old attitudes of paternalism" and "to promote partnership and self-help." He added, "Our goal must be: A standard of living for Indians equal to that of the country as a whole, freedom of choice—and opportunity to remain in their homeland, if they choose, without surrendering their dignity, and an opportunity to move to the towns and cities of America if they choose, equipped with skills to live in equality and dignity; full participation in the life of modern America, with a full share of economic and social justice."

Unfortunately, this utopian vision has not come to pass. Consider one of the banes of Indian existence: alcohol. As early as 1786, Bernardo de Gálvez's *Instructions* had included liquor

A group of Apache boys play basketball at a reservation school. During the 1960s, President Lyndon B. Johnson proposed that the U.S. government should not try to assimilate Native Americans into mainstream society but rather allow them to follow their own beliefs and practices.

among the items Indians should be given free as a means of weakening them. In 1850, Mexicans plotted the Ramos massacre by inviting Apaches to a long drinking bout that left them helpless. American traders regularly plied Indians with whiskey or rum in order to fleece them of valuable goods. Indeed, alcohol became so potent a weapon that in 1802 the U.S. Congress passed the Trade and Intercourse Act. Its main provision authorized President Thomas Jefferson (1801–09) to regulate and even prohibit the sale of spirits to Indians, not as punishment but as a means of protection against swindlers.

Yet alcoholism continued to plague American Indians throughout the nineteenth century and well into the twentieth. In recent years, the U.S. government has tried to discourage alcohol abuse among Indians—as well as among other groups—but with negligible success. Statistics released in 1983 by the U.S. Department of Health and Human Services showed that the percentage of alcohol-related deaths among American Indians was nearly five times the figure for other ethnic groups. A report issued in 1985 by the Indian Health Service concluded that death from alcoholism among Indians between the ages of 25 and 34 occurred 11.2 times more frequently than for all other Americans of the same age. Among those between the ages of 35 and 44, the rate is 7.7 percent higher; among those between the ages of 45 and 54, the rate is 4.8 percent higher.

The various twentieth-century Apache bands have struggled valiantly to overcome hardship against odds no less imposing than those they faced in earlier times. Consider the case of the Western Apaches. In the early 1900s, many of the 1,811 Western Apaches estimated to live on the Fort Apache Reservation gave up their effort to live off the land and began to work for wages. In 1907, the U.S. Army employed eighty men to cut hay for horses, as Lieutenant Whitman had done thirty-six years before. Dozens more worked as cowboys. In 1918, the Apaches were encouraged to begin cattle ranching, and by 1931 they owned more than 20,000 head. In the 1980s, cattle raising remained a major industry on the San Carlos and Fort Apache reservations. Another industry, lumber, attracted the Apaches in the 1920s and has become a major source of income, employing 200 men and processing 50 million feet of board per year. In the 1950s, a third type of business—outdoor recreation—emerged as a mainstay of Apache employment, as the people drew on time-honored skills to develop camping areas and build cabins.

This income enabled the people to bolster their food supply. They bought flour, coffee, sugar, and beans and added these goods to their traditional diet. Many Apaches, however, continue to live in dire poverty on the Fort Apache Reservation. A study conducted in 1969 indicated that 49 percent of the

Apaches living on the reservation earned less than $1,000 annually, including welfare payments—vastly below the national average. Eighty percent of Apache homes fell below normal standards—90 percent lacked heat, 74 percent lacked indoor plumbing, and 46 percent had no electricity. The average house had only two rooms.

The Mescaleros have not fared much better. In 1881, U.S. General John Pope declared: "It is idle to talk of civilizing the Mescalero Apaches. They are savages, pure and simple, and in the country they occupy, with the inducements to raid and the present management of the tribe, it is worse than childish to believe that they are being, or ever will be, reclaimed." Three years later a priest from Lincoln County, New Mexico, tried to introduce the band to Christianity and baptized 173 people. The next year the U.S. government established a Court of Indian Offenses, run by the Mescaleros themselves, who held judicial hearings, passed verdicts, and issued sentences.

Still, the Mescaleros sought to preserve their customary life. They settled in isolated groups and observed their traditional habits as much as possible. At the end of the nineteenth century, the U.S. government redoubled its efforts to "civilize" the band. American officials supervised a reservation on a wagon road along the Tularosa Canyon, near present-day Mescalero, New Mexico, off Interstate 70. Eventually, the Mescaleros began to settle in town, and other Apaches joined them. By 1915, leaders of the local groups were meeting with BIA officials, and in 1936 the Mescaleros proclaimed a tribal constitution under the terms of the Indian Reorganization Act (IRA), passed by Congress in 1934. This bill empowered the newly created tribal governments to negotiate with federal, state, and local authorities. The IRA attempted to weaken the vast power of the BIA and to restore some autonomy to Indians. As was the case with the Western Apaches, Indian agents assumed that agriculture would provide the economic base for reservation life. Yet water was scarce in the Tularosa Canyon. Enough existed to irrigate

The Inn of the Mountain Gods, which was built in the 1970s and renovated in 2005, is one of the Mescaleros' most profitable sources of income. The resort, located on the Mescalero Apache Reservation, has an on-site casino and offers golf, skiing, and big-game hunting.

only three hundred acres. Agents next promoted raising sheep and goats, but the land lacked vegetation for grazing. Cattle ranching suited the terrain better, but the income it produced could not support the Mescaleros. They added to it marginally by cutting timber.

Reservation life proved so unrewarding that in 1946 the annual income for one-third of reservation Indians averaged less than $500, while the other two-thirds lived on less than $1,000. In recent times, the Mescaleros have turned to tourism and recreation as a means of improving their standard of living. They have developed a resort hotel—the Inn of the Mountain Gods—golf courses, an industrial park, and other enterprises in New Mexico.

The band's population has increased slightly. In 1988, the Mescaleros numbered about 1,700. Unemployment remains a problem. As much as 70 percent of the workforce were without jobs during the lean years of the 1970s and 1980s. Education is one solution. In 1972, nineteen Mescaleros were attending college, and the number has increased since then.

Destitution also marked the early reservation days of the Jicarillas. Again, the area they were given—the Jicarilla Reservation in northern New Mexico—proved unsuitable for agriculture. Also, the climate and limited acreage made cattle raising difficult until the U.S. government enlarged the reservation in 1907. Timber harvesting did not provide a realistic alternative because of legal complications and confusion about policy. Disease and malnutrition took their toll. From 1905 to 1920 the band's population declined from 995 to 588. In 1917, the Indian agent reported that 90 percent of the school-aged population suffered from tuberculosis.

The U.S. government finally acted in 1920, and within a decade health improved on the reservation as tuberculosis was brought under control. Sheep raising proved a viable industry—as an individual rather than collective enterprise. Some Jicarillas turned a profit and the standard of living rose. Like the Mescaleros, the Jicarillas organized a tribal government in 1937 under the terms of the IRA. They also established a tribal corporation to direct the reservation's economy. Income from livestock rose, along with health standards and the size of the population.

Sheepherding remained the mainstay of the band through the 1940s and the reservation's natural resources provided a substantial income. Gas, oil, and timber reserves were all abundant. The Jicarillas managed to turn these resources to their advantage and phased out sheepherding. No reason remained for living off the land, and they moved in increasing numbers to Dulce, the agency headquarters. By 1954, 80 percent of the Jicarillas lived within seven miles of the agency.

Like other groups, the Jicarillas tried to assert more control over their own affairs and formed a governmental council. The BIA, however, still regulated their lives. The council usually rubber-stamped federal programs and carried them out with Apache funds. Although the Apaches have struggled valiantly to adjust to the American way of life, its underlying philosophy continues to seem alien to them. Americans showed no understanding of, among other things, the southwestern landscape. The Apaches revered everything that grew on the desert, including the century plant. This unique plant stores nourishment for fifteen years, then thrusts a six-foot stalk into the air, from which pollen is scattered. The stalk then topples and the plant dies—a cruel fate, but one expressive of the region. The Apaches understood that nature did not overflow with generosity. Mere survival required enormous effort.

The Apaches traditionally accepted life on the terms offered by nature. They felt no need to tame it, to batter it into submission, to despoil its deserts and deplete its resources. They were born of the land, and they lived by its rules. But the newcomers thought otherwise. The Spaniards viewed the land materially, as property and as the instruments for their private projects and dreams of power and wealth. Estevanico escaped servitude and tricked himself out in finery. Coronado dreamed of glorious conquest and riches. The Americans were equally stricken with avarice. Many lusted for gold, silver, and other ore deposits that could be gouged out of the soil. This craving lured them to the southwest, where they thoughtlessly killed buffalo, which for some of the Apaches had been a source of food, clothing, and tools. Similarly, the Americans had no qualms about driving the Apaches off their ancestral homelands and destroying their communities. As Frank Lockwood wrote in *Pioneer Days in Arizona*, "Every [white] man had in his heart a burning desire to kill an Apache wherever he could find him."

The arid deserts and forested mountains of the American Southwest were once filled with the Apaches. They fought to hold onto their bounty even as they were overrun by white people of various nationalities, who coveted their land and reduced them to a subject people. They struggled to retain their traditional way of life—their customs, ceremonies, folklore, and beliefs.

In recent times, the Apaches have been trapped between the past and the present. Yet the Apache heritage testifies eloquently to their strength. Like the century plant, this heritage will inevitably blossom and cast its seeds into the soil. Many of them will take root and grow.

7

The Apache Nations in the Twenty-First Century

In 2005, nine different groups of Native Americans continue to identify themselves as Apache. Most Apaches reside on five reservations in Arizona and New Mexico: White Mountain Apaches (Fort Apache Indian Reservation), San Carlos Apaches, Tonto Apaches, Yavapai-Apache Nation (Camp Verde Reservation), and the Fort McDowell Yavapai Nation (formerly the Fort McDowell Mohave-Apaches). The second-largest number live in New Mexico, on the Jicarilla Apache and Mescalero Apache reservations. Smaller groups reside in Texas, the Lipan Apaches, and in Oklahoma, the Fort Sill Apaches. Apaches are also scattered throughout the United States, living off their reservation while retaining an Apache identity. Although divided by geography, ceremonial expressions of culture, and political orientation, all of these groups share common problems and a common identity as Apache, as Native Americans, and as Americans.

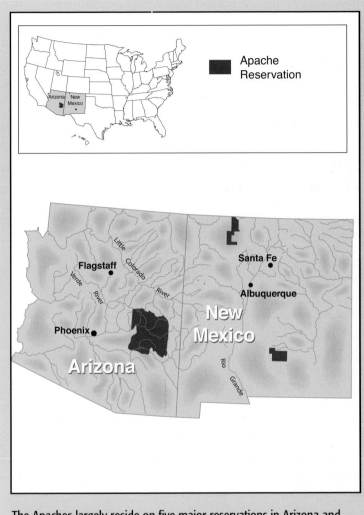

The Apaches largely reside on five major reservations in Arizona and New Mexico. According to the 2000 U.S. Census, there are more than 57,000 Apaches who live in the United States.

Like most Native Americans, as the Apaches entered the twenty-first century they struggled with the legacy of misconceptions of the nineteenth century and the economic difficulties of the twentieth century. U.S. Army helicopters called the Apache reflected a sense of the Apaches' fierce military prowess, while reinforcing the notion that Apaches were violent warriors. High school sports teams continued to use the Apache as a team name and as mascots, objectifying them in the process. Some progress has been made, however, in combating stereotypes. In one case, Arcadia High School officials in California invited Apache tribal representatives to discuss Apache life and culture with Arcadia students, eventually replacing a cartoonish "Apache Joe" logo with a more authentic Apache image, and sending its band to perform on the Apache Reservation. Although the Apaches have made valiant

The Achesnay Memorial Hall Controversy

In October 1972, a controversy began to brew on the White Mountain Apache Reservation. The tribal council moved to change the name of Achesnay Memorial Hall, which honored the last Apache "chief" of the nineteenth century, to Ralph Aday Memorial Hall, which would have honored a young Apache soldier who lost his life during World War II. The council thought the change befitted "the memory of Apaches who had lost their lives while serving their country." According to the reservation newspaper, the *Apache Scout*, a considerable number of Apaches, including Geronimo's great-grandson, condemned the proposed name change, in part because Achesnay was "a legend." The council's apparently minor decision to rename a communal building mushroomed into a big debate about whose—and which—version of the Apache past would be accepted. On the surface it appeared that many Apaches defended a figure who defined nineteenth-century Apache nationalism rather than one who represented modern America. But Achesnay was noted largely for his service to the United States in the 1886 capture of Geronimo, a symbol of final resistance to American domination. This incident nicely illustrates the complex and layered ways in which Native Americans have wrestled with their history and their identity as both Native and American. It shows that the Apaches, and Native Americans in general, balanced their loyalty to the United States and to the tribe in a dual patriotism that is reinforcing.

strides in overcoming stereotypes and misunderstanding, they are still fighting discrimination and neglect. When wildfires were devastating parts of the American West during the summer of 2002, a front page article in the *New York Times* noted that "[w]hile national attention is focused on the threat Arizona's wildfires pose to Show Low, the [white] resort town, the blaze has already brought widespread and lasting economic damage to Apache country . . . Little emergency aid has been sent to White River, the seat of tribal government, though 1,500 Apaches have been evacuated from their homes."

In the early 1970s, Apache groups of New Mexico, Arizona, and Oklahoma began to work together to solve problems that affect *all* Apaches rather than only individual tribal groups, which has reinforced ideas of common cultural heritage. Apache efforts to reclaim ancestral remains and tribal art and objects from museums and the federal government, a process known as repatriation, especially helped to unify Apache communities. In November 1995, the various bands of Apaches gathered at an *All-Apache Summit* to address problems with the repatriation process. The Summit produced the All-Apache Culture Committee, whose mission was to "oversee and act as an advocate for traditional cultural preservation and the repatriation of Apache cultural items and property." According to Ramon Riley, a Tribal Heritage Program director, the meeting was very productive. "We all thought something like this would never happen. It gives us a tool to work together. Now we're united to fight [discrimination]." Similar gatherings have taken place since 1995. The All-Apache Summit of July 12–14, 2004, drew one hundred participants from eight Apache nations to discuss shortcomings in national repatriation legislation called the *Native American Graves Protection and Repatriation Act* (NAGPRA), renew the Apache Bill of Rights, and create an All-Apache Heritage Center to demonstrate the cultural links between the various Apache tribes.

This effort to preserve Apache identity through culture also occurs on each reservation. The mission statement of the Jicarilla Apache Cultural Center is that the Center "promotes, protects and perpetuates the living culture of the Jicarilla Apache Nation by educating the community, public and tribal membership." In a two-hundred-page document outlining its cultural revitalization and preservation agenda, the cultural center staff vowed that "Aba'Achi migoya'meedasi nzho'go me ch'aa kai,'" which means in English, "The Apache will lead forward by strong and beautiful thoughts." The cultural center pursues this mission on the strength of advice from traditional and spiritual leaders, both male and female, of the Jicarilla Culture Committee, which was established in November 1993 to "provide the necessary expertise and advice on all matters that relate to the traditions and culture." Roughly two hundred Jicarilla elders still speak in the Jicarilla Apache language. Jicarilla (pronounced hek-a-REH-ya) means "little basket," which relates to the skillful Apache basket weavers. The Jicarillas have three main ceremonies: the Jicarilla Day Pow-Wow in February, the Little Beaver celebration in late July, which includes a rodeo, powwow, parade, and dances, and the Go-Jii Yah Feast, a September thanksgiving celebration of races, powwows, and rodeos. Non-Apaches are invited to attend these events but need to follow protocols that respect tribal traditions.

The White Mountain Apaches have a similar mission in maintaining their White Mountain Apache cultural center and museum, or "Nohwike' Bagowa," which means "House of our Footprints" in the Apache language. Established in 1969, the cultural center and museum preserves Apache cultural artifacts and history and offers non-Apaches a chance to trace the history of the White Mountain Apaches through exhibits, educational programs, and archival materials. A recent exhibit called *Tus* and *Tats'aa* explored the role of basketry in Apache life and history. The White Mountain Apaches also try

The Sunrise Ceremony remains a fixture of Apache culture, even in today's modern world. Shown here is a girl who has just been painted by her godfather, signifying the moment when she officially becomes a woman.

to foster Apache spirituality in the form of *Bini' godilkqqh* (smoothness of mind), *bini' gonil'iz* (resilience of mind), and *bini gonldzil* (steadiness of mind).

The White Mountain Apaches continue to hold sacred Sunrise Dances, the initiation ceremony for Apache girls aged eleven to thirteen years old. As relatives, friends, and community members look on, a medicine man and "Crown Dancers" bless the girl. The ceremony, which lasts several days, strengthens the girl's physical and psychological strength to help prepare her for womanhood. The Mescalero Apaches also maintain important ceremonies, such as the "Coming Out" festival for Apache girls. Non-Apaches are invited to attend other festival events like the Dance of the Mountain Gods and a

Fourth of July rodeo and parade, an example of how Native Americans practice American events in a Native way.

While some of the ceremonies mark old traditions, such as the Sunrise Dances, or offer an Apache version of an American celebration, such as the Fourth of July, some newer ceremonies recognize the accomplishments of modern Apaches. For example, each November the Fort McDowell Yavapai-Apaches mark their success in defeating the federal government's Orme Dam project with their Orme Dam Victory Days Celebration at the Fort McDowell Rodeo Grounds; the Fort McDowell Yavapai-Apaches also celebrate their ability to maintain important elements of political sovereignty with their annual May Sovereignty Day Celebration.

Apaches are very protective of their land and the places where their history comes from. "Wisdom sits in places," says Dudley Patterson, a White Mountain Apache. Preserving culture for the Apaches means preserving the reservation. Apaches for Cultural Preservation was founded by San Carlos Apaches Wendsler Nosie Sr. and Ernest Victor Jr. to teach young Apaches "to preserve what is left, such as traditional ceremonies, songs, language, foods, spirituality, and sacred sites." Nosie and Victor have organized an annual Mt. Graham Sacred Run to protest what they see are violations of a sacred Apache site called Mt. Graham, which houses an observatory used by various universities, including the University of Arizona. According to Apaches for Cultural Preservation, "Mt. Graham is the home of our Angels, the Gahn." The annual run starts with sweat lodge purification ceremonies and blessings. Runners come from various Apache reservations and from other Native American communities and also include non-Indian supporters from American states, and from France, Algeria, Denmark, and Italy.

Apaches hope to educate non-Indians with these various exhibits, ceremonies, and events but mainly to reinforce among Apache youth the importance of culture in their lives. Apache schools have worked to combine cultural education with the kind of learning necessary for economic advancement in the twenty-first century. Each Apache nation provides various educational opportunities to its members. White Mountain Apaches attend public school in the Whiteriver Unified School District or in the Cibecue Community School. They can also attend the Theodore Roosevelt School and the John F. Kennedy School, which are operated by the Bureau of Indian Affairs. In public schools that comprise Apache and non-Apache students, some Apaches have started special clubs, such as the San Carlos Native American club.

The various Apache communities benefit from Head Start programs and the Child Care and Development Block Grant (CCDBG) program, which is a main source of support for communities that cannot afford good child care. Some of the Apache schools integrate Apache language programs into their curriculum. For example, the Fort McDowell Yavapai-Apaches run the 'Hman' shawa Elementary School, paying for it exclusively with tribal funds. Its focus is to balance American-style education with Apache language and culture classes. The school's motto is: "Our children . . . the center of everything."

After graduating high school, many Apaches attend Arizona's state universities, as well as the local Northland Pioneer College in Whiteriver, the capital of the White Mountain Apache Nation. In recent years, their students have done very well in higher education, helped by a challenge from a director of the National Native American Honor Society, which recognizes straight-A students from Native American communities. Rising to the challenge to produce better students, Wesley Bonito and other tribal leaders organized a meeting with honor society representatives to work out a plan for improving educational success through teacher, parent, and honor society leaders. The result: White Mountain Apaches raised the number of "classroom warriors" eligible for membership in the society from 8 in 1992 to 180 in 1997, generating great pride and new role models.

Many of these college graduates contribute to the modernization of the Apache reservation economies by managing tribal development programs, running businesses, or serving on political bodies that help to generate new businesses. Most Apaches adapted to reservation life by grazing livestock and operating small farms, growing pumpkins, beans, apples, and corn. Cowboy life remains popular among many Apaches. On the WMA, eight cattle associations of between 40 and 70 members tended to 1,500 to 2,000 head of cattle. There is even an "Old Folks' Herd" maintained by the tribe for the benefit of Apache elders; a small staff of White Mountain Apaches help to take care of about 2,100 cattle. Such cooperative ventures speak to the retention of community-oriented economic development among Apaches and among Native Americans generally.

Beginning in the 1960s, tribal leaders began to expand economic opportunities, arguing that an important way to preserve Apache culture was to provide economic stability. For example, the San Carlos Apache Nation started its Apache Nation Chamber of Commerce in 2000 to "create environments that ensure the greatest opportunity for success and self-sufficiency of our members and communities." San Carlos businesses include restaurants, markets, arts and crafts shops, livestock, tourist-related companies, as well as the Apache Gold Casino Resort.

All Arizona Apache nations have a casino, as do the Mescaleros and Jicarillas in New Mexico. Fundamentally, casinos have provided employment opportunities, job-training, and income. As in other Native American nations, Apache governments use casino revenues to fund social services for the elderly, provide educational opportunities like college scholarships for the young, and help to develop long-term economic development programs for all Apache citizens.

Supported by revenue generated from casinos, as well as by Small Business Administration loans, the Apaches have been enterprising. The White Mountain Apaches (WMA) started the Sunrise Park Resort, which now boasts some of the best skiing in Arizona and in the Southwest generally, offering sixty-five trails and separate snowboarding and cross-country skiing areas, along with a lodge, and a summer marina. The White Mountain Apaches' Hon-Dah Resort-Casino and Conference Center offers a range of summer activities, as well as year-round gaming.

After World War II, the WMA aggressively developed the reservation's natural resources. In 1954, tribal leaders formed the WMA Recreational Enterprise to attract non-Indians from the arid and hot desert-like conditions of the Phoenix area to the cool mountains of the reservation. As Phoenix and the White Mountain Apache communities grew in size, they began to compete over the same resources. The WMA sued the State of Arizona in 1983 for violating the terms of use of the Salt River, which provides water to reservations.

The White Mountain Apaches, whose name comes from a range of mountains on the Fort Apache Indian Reservation, have a rich supply of forest resources. Nearly three-fifths of the reservation contains timber, much of it commercial quality. WMA have become leaders in managing multiple-use forests. In addition to harvesting timber, the White Mountain Apaches have fish and wildlife management programs that offer elk hunting, the licenses of which can cost more than $10,000.

Importantly, Apache tribal leaders took control of these resources after non-Indians benefitted from them for decades. The White Mountain Apache tribal timber enterprise, called the Fort Apache Timber Company (FATCo), began operation in 1963 and by 1968 the tribal council was no longer granting contracts to non-Apaches. After building their own sawmills, over the next two decades the tribe earned $52.5 million in revenues through FATCo's operations, making it one of the largest timber operators in the United States. It is also staffed primarily by Apache workers and is currently associated with Western Wood Products Association, a trade-group organization centered in Oregon. While the number of White Mountain Apaches working on the reservation has grown apace, the unemployment rate has risen, from 22.8 percent in 1990 to 27.3 percent in 2003.

Under the leadership of Wendell Chino, the Mescalero Apaches also expanded reservation businesses. In the 1970s, the Mescalero Apache Tribal Council (MATC) created the Inn of the Mountain Gods Resort and Casino, which offers golf, skiing, and a ski school at Ski Apache, big-game hunting, and wedding and conference facilities. Making good use of its natural resources, the Mescaleros also started the Mescalero National Fish Hatchery, though a flood in 2003 virtually wiped out 230,000 rainbow trout that were headed to streams and lakes of other Indian nations in the Southwest, including other Apache nations. Mescalero businesses also include infrastructure services like Mescalero Gas Company and Mescalero Apache Telecom Inc. In September 2000, Mescalero Apache Telecom Inc. (MATI) became the seventh Native American phone company to receive regulatory approval nationwide and the first in New Mexico. A MATI spokesman stated that the new service will enable Apache citizens to gain access to DSL (Digital Subscriber Lines) lines. It will also improve the phone service and high-speed Internet connections for major Mescalero businesses, such as the Inn of the Mountain Gods and Casino Apache, which depend on non-Apache tourists. MATI will help the Mescaleros get more grants and loans and to become more self-sufficient.

The Jicarilla Apache is one of the wealthiest Indian nations in the country, largely because of its oil and gas operations, which began producing significant revenue in the 1970s. Like other Apache nations, the Jicarilla has aggressively sought to maintain control of resource development projects. To take

Mark Chino, who was elected president of the Mescalero Apaches in 2003, signs a bill in 2004 that paid the State of New Mexico $25 million for back revenues it would have received from the Mescaleros' Casino Apache. As part of the agreement with the state, the Mescaleros must share 8 percent of the annual revenues they receive from Casino Apache.

advantage of their reservation mineral resources, the Jicarillas formed the Jicarilla Energy Company in the 1980s to ensure that the bulk of oil and gas revenues went to the Jicarilla people. For twenty years, the Jicarilla government has also bought adjoining land to strengthen the boundaries of the reservation. While some Jicarillas have complained that more of these revenues should be given to the people directly in the form of per-capita payments, others celebrate the development—since the year 2000—of a new elementary school, a new library, and a new health clinic that doubled the staff and improved the medical technology available to Jicarilla citizens. In Dulce, the reservation capital, Jicarilla businesses include a bowling alley, a fitness center, a swimming pool, a shopping center, and a lighted softball field.

The Apaches have been at the center of important legal cases that have decided the ways that Native Americans everywhere have defined their sovereignty. For example, in the 1982 case of *Merrion v. Jicarilla Apache Tribe*, the U.S. Supreme Court ruled that non-Indian companies had to pay taxes to the Indian tribes on whose reservations they were doing business. In 1983, in *New Mexico v. Mescalero Apache*, the Supreme Court ruled that the Mescaleros, and thus all Indians, could set the rules and regulations for non-Indians hunting and fishing on their reservation, not the state governments.

Aggressively asserting their sovereignty, the Mescaleros became involved in a controversial economic development program in the 1990s. In 1982, Congress passed the Nuclear Waste Policy Act (NWPA), which established an agenda for dealing with the ever-increasing amount of spent fuel rods and other radioactive wastes that nuclear power plants produce. A 1987 amendment to the Act funded the search for a community to accept Monitored Retrievable Storage (MRS) facilities to hold, temporarily, radioactive materials until a permanent site at Yucca Mountain, Nevada, could be built. In December 1992, U.S. Nuclear Waste Negotiator David Leroy offered Native American communities $100,000 just to consider participation in the MRS program. Mescalero Apache politicians were the first to receive the $100,000 grant, dividing the Mescalero people among pro-dump and anti-dump forces. Mescalero Apache Tribal Council (MATC) president Wendell Chino considered the nuclear storage proposal "a business opportunity" worth considering because "people need the work." Chino noted that it would require round-the-clock guards, technicians, and other professional jobs and could possibly generate between $15 and 25 million per year in revenues; he argued that "the storage of spent nuclear fuel is a twenty-first century industry with the attendant complement of high-tech, high-wage jobs not often available to Indian tribes."

Under Chino's guidance, the MATC went through the first two stages of the MRS permit process before applying for a $2.8 million grant. Mescelaro Apache Rufina Marie Laws started Humans Against Nuclear Waste Dumps to oppose MATC's nuclear waste storage proposal. Laws' organization quickly networked with other Native American groups facing similar battles. According to Laws, "As I met more people concerned with this issue, I realized that it takes on a much broader scope than just the Apaches. We are giving support to other Native American groups across the country that are facing this issue." Laws has become a national leader for Native Americans opposed to using their land for the dumping of nuclear and hazardous wastes. Laws had an important ally in Joseph Geronimo, the great-grandson of the famous Apache leader Geronimo, a symbol of nineteenth-century resistance to American domination. Displaying a tenacity that would make his great-grandfather proud, he explained his vote against the MRS plan proposed by the Mescalero Apache Tribal Council by saying, "Very few of us will be around forty years from now. Our children will be stuck with it. And what would they get for it? Nothing? Our people have made the choice that their tradition and culture is the most important thing in the world, and Grandmother Earth is not for sale at any price." After a long battle, Mescalero Apache voters defeated the tribal council's MRS proposal.

Wendell Chino's death of a heart attack at seventy-four years of age in November 1998 stunned the Mescalero community. Chino had been on the tribal council since it was formed in 1965 and had helped lead the tribe for thirty-three years; he was elected to seventeen consecutive terms as council president. "He was always thinking of our children—education— and making businesses big. He was making sure the tribe will exist, making sure the Apache people stay strong and together,

Former Mescalero Apache president Wendell Chino addresses the state senate in Santa Fe, New Mexico, in 1996. Chino, who died in 1998, served as president of his tribe from 1965 until his death, was an advocate of self-determination, and helped generate economic opportunities for his people.

and teaching tribal history to our children," said Zenda Kaydahzinne. Chino secured public housing funds for the reservation in the 1960s, asserted Mescalero sovereignty in important court cases in the 1970s and 1980s, and helped generate economic opportunities for his people. Chino always championed Indian sovereignty and land rights. In 1977, he said:

> Our people are on the move. We are developing our people and lands so that we and our children can participate wholly in the full American way. We want to continue to improve the social, political, economic and educational development of our people while at the same time preserving tribal autonomy. As American Indians we have been grossly wronged, hurt and abused, but we cannot linger on the past. For too

long other people have been telling us what is good for us. Let us make America believe that the American Indian is the final arbiter of his own future.

The Mescalero situation reflects a heightened sense of political participation on the part of all Apache tribal members, who have pushed for legal changes that restored elements of sovereignty to their individual nations. Apache tribal governments are regulated and defined by tribal constitutions, and express their political power in executive, legislative, and judicial branches. Apache politics, like U.S. politics in general, are contested by various constituencies. Reservation politics, especially those that have to do with economic policies, have generated controversies and accusations of corruption and voter fraud. Apache efforts to assert their economic sovereignty by operating casinos, though allowed by the federal government, have also created tensions with state governments intent on regulating that sovereignty and claiming revenues from those casinos.

Some of the strongest advocates of Apache sovereignty are women. The Apache puberty ceremony for girls speaks of their belief in the strong power of women and the important roles they play in maintaining the community. This belief is reflected in the political makeup of Apache political bodies. Three members of the six-person Oklahoma Fort Sill Apache business committee are women. Four women help to make up the six-person Fort McDowell Yavapai-Apache tribal government. In 2003, a woman, Claudia Vigil-Muniz, was elected as the president of the Jicarilla Apache Nation, and Stacey Sanchez served as the spokesperson of the president. In 1999, Sara Misquez was elected to serve as president of the Mescalero Apache Tribal Council. A year later, Misquez addressed the New Mexico state legislature, asking lawmakers to "set aside old stereotypes and begin a new chapter in our governmental relations." Other Mescalero Apache women

Claudia Vigil-Muniz, shown here preparing for a tribal council meeting, was elected the Jicarilla Apaches' first female president in 2003. Vigil-Muniz formerly worked in the tribe's department of education.

served in important political roles, such as councilwoman and Election Board chairperson. Women also occupy important positions in legal affairs and cultural affairs departments. On the Jicarilla Apache Reservation, for example, Bernice Muskrat and Teresa Luger de Fernandez serve as tribal attorneys, while Lorene Willis directs the Jicarilla Apache Cultural Affairs office. Apache women play an integral role in helping to shape a politics based on a historical foundation of Apache culture.

Like many Americans in rural parts of the United States, members of these various Apache communities suffer from high rates of poverty, alcoholism, crime, and inadequate health care. The Apaches, like other Native Americas, also suffer from higher unemployment rates than in non-Indian communities.

These are significant problems that Apaches struggle to address, using both Apache and American solutions. Like many Native Americans across the country, Apaches partake in the larger American culture. Apache teenagers wear jeans and use the Internet. The Apaches, like many Americans, are mad about basketball. They play "hoops" at all educational levels, and each June they had their own tournament, the Native American Invitation Tournament.

Apaches also work hard to maintain what is distinctly Apache—their language, their traditional ceremonies, their kinship networks that tie various clans together, and their commitment to Apache land. They display these cultural commitments in public festivals and in most cases want non-Apaches to visit them, to hear their stories, see some of their ceremonies, and get to know them as people having common interests, problems, and goals like anyone else. As Mescalero Apache Nation president Sara Misquez told New Mexico state legislators on Indian Day, February 2000, "Our futures, whether we realize it or not, are most assuredly intertwined."

Apaches also have distinct interests—including repatriation, sovereignty, economic development, and water rights—that affect their ability to define themselves as Apache in the twenty-first century. The Apaches fight for their right to be Apache, together and as individual nations, in ways that are decidedly American, by participating in the democratic process, by negotiating with state and federal governments, and by drawing upon the collective intellectual and cultural wealth of their communities.

The Apaches at a Glance

Tribe	Apache
Culture Area	Southwest
Geography	Primarily Arizona and New Mexico
Linguistic Family	Athapaskan
Current Population (2000)	More than 57,000
First European Contact	Cabeza de Vaca, Spanish, 1534
Federal Status	The Apaches live on five major reservations. Two are located in New Mexico and the others in Arizona. Each reservation has a tribal government established under the Indian Reorganization Act of 1934

1542 Francisco Vásquez de Coronado claims much of the American Southwest in the name of Spain.

1785–1821 War between Spanish troops and the Apaches.

1848 Treaty of Guadalupe Hidalgo ends the Mexican War; U.S. annexes New Mexico Territory (including Arizona).

1849 Jicarilla Apaches and Utes attack U.S. troops at the Cimarron River cutoff of the Santa Fe Trail.

1851 Jicarillas and Mescaleros sign treaty with James S. Calhoun, governor of New Mexico Territory.

1852 Apache leader Mangas begins raids on U.S. interests.

1854 Governor of New Mexico Territory declares war on the Jicarillas.

1860 Chiricahuas begin twenty-five-year war with U.S. government.

1862 U.S. Army establishes Fort Bowie in Apache Pass.

1863 Mangas tortured and shot by U.S. Army soldiers.

1871 A mob of white vigilantes from Tucson ambush a group of Apaches promised protection by the U.S. Army. The murder of Apaches and the kidnapping of twenty-eight Apache children becomes known as the Camp Grant Massacre.

1872 U.S. government establishes five Apache reservations—four in Arizona, one in New Mexico; Chiricahua leader Cochise signs peace treaty with United States creating the Chiricahua Reservation.

1876 U.S. abolishes Chiricahua Reservation and forcibly relocates the Chiricahuas to the San Carlos Reservation.

1877–1880 Victorio leads resistance to U.S. policies.

1886 Geronimo surrenders to General Nelson Miles after resisting U.S. domination for six years.

1890 All Apache bands settled on U.S. government reservations.

1909   Geronimo dies at Fort Sill, Oklahoma.

1918   Apaches begin to raise cattle.

1936   Mescalero, San Carlos, and Fort McDowell Mohave Apaches adopt an Indian Reorganization Act government and constitution.

1937   Jicarilla Apaches and Yavapai-Apache Indian Community adopt an Indian Reorganization Act government and constitution.

1938   White Mountain Apaches adopt an Indian Reorganization Act government and constitution.

1973   "The Apache Bill of Rights" adopted to recognize "close Apache kinship" and find "common cause" between the various Apache groups.

1982   U.S. Supreme Court decides case of *Merrion v. Jicarilla Apache Tribe* in favor of the Jicarillas, and other Indian nations, ruling that non-Indian companies had to pay taxes to the Indian tribes on whose reservations they were doing business.

1983   In *New Mexico v. Mescalero Apache*, the Supreme Court ruled that the Mescaleros, and thus all Indians, could set the rules and regulations for non-Indians hunting and fishing on their reservation, not the state governments.

1995   All-Apache Culture Committee formed to work on cultural issues common to all Apache groups.

1997   The Apache Survival Coalition asks the Ninth U.S. Circuit Court of Appeals to prevent construction of telescopes on Mt. Graham (Arizona), considered sacred to the Apaches.

All-Apache Summit—Gathering of Apache tribes to address common economic and political problems. The original summit adopted the "The Apache Bill of Rights," which affirmed "the unity of our Apache nation."

Apache—Nomadic, Athapaskan-speaking Native American peoples of the American Southwest and Mexico.

Apachean Tribal Groups—The divisions of the Apache Indians that include the Jicarillas, Lipans, Kiowa-Apaches, Chiricahuas, Mescaleros, and Western Apaches.

Athapaskan—Among Native Americans, the most widely dispersed linguistic family. Athapaskan speakers such as the Apaches can be found not only in the Southwest but also along the Northwest coast, Alaska, and Canada.

Aztec—A race of Native Americans that established an empire in Mexico.

band—The smallest, simplest type of politically independent society that occupies a specific territory.

breechcloth—A strip of cloth worn around the hips and groin.

Bureau of Indian Affairs (BIA)—A U.S. government agency established in 1824 and assigned to the Department of the Interior in 1849. Originally intended to manage trade and other relations with Indians and especially to supervise tribes on reservations, the BIA is now involved in programs that encourage Indians to manage their own affairs and improve their educational opportunities and general social and economic well-being.

Child of the Water—The son of sky god Life Giver and White-painted Woman. He is considered the father of the Apaches.

clan—A multigenerational group having a shared identity, organization, and property and based on the belief in descent from a common ancestor. Because clan members consider themselves closely related, marriage within the clan is strictly prohibited.

Federally Recognized Tribes—Indian tribes recognized by the federal government as self-governing entities with which the United States maintains a government-to-government political relationship. Recognized tribes are eligible for special services and benefits designated solely for such tribes (for example, BIA programs, Indian Health Services).

Gadsden Purchase—An 1853 agreement between the United States and Mexico in which Mexico gave up the southern parts of Arizona and New Mexico in return for $10 million.

GLOSSARY

Gran Apacheria—The Spanish term for Apache territory. It included New Mexico and parts of Texas, Colorado, Kansas, Arizona, Oklahoma, and northern Mexico.

Guadalupe Hidalgo, Treaty of—The 1848 agreement that ended the war between the United States and Mexico. In exchange for $15 million, Mexico agreed to accept the Rio Grande as the southern border of Texas and to cede the territories of California and New Mexico to the United States.

Indian Gaming Regulatory Act (IGRA)—Congress passed the IGRA in 1988 to provide the statutory basis for the administration of Indian gaming businesses. The IGRA created the National Indian Gaming Commission to oversee these businesses.

Indian Mineral Development Act (IMDA)—Congress passed the IMDA in 1982 to facilitate the expansion of Native American energy production. The Jicarilla Apaches formed a tribal energy corporation in 1982.

Killer of Enemies—Considered by some Apachean groups to be the primary cultural hero instead of Child of the Water.

Lakota—Native Americans who inhabited the plains of Nebraska, North and South Dakota, and Wyoming.

Life Giver—Sky god or the god of the sky. In Apache mythology, he was credited with creating the universe.

Masked Dancer—Supernatural being called upon in curing ceremonies.

mescal—A type of liquor distilled from maguey plants.

nantà—Apachean term for leader.

Native American Graves Protection and Repatriation Act (NAGPRA)—The legislation, passed in 1990, established new codes for protecting Native American gravesites and set guidelines for federal agencies and museums receiving federal funding to return sacred objects, ancestral remains, or cultural patrimony (defined as objects "having ongoing historical, traditional, or cultural importance, central to the Native American group or culture itself").

N'de, Dinï, Tindé, or Indé—The terms, translated as "the people," by which the Apaches call themselves.

Pawnee—Native Americans of the Caddoan-speaking family. They inhabited the Platte River valley of Nebraska.

Pima—A division of Native Americans living in the Salt and Gila river valleys.

GLOSSARY

Power—In Apachean religion, a good and/or evil force that affects human lives.

presidio—A Spanish term for fort.

pueblo—A Spanish term for a town or village of certain southwestern Indians; also the name of the group of Indian peoples of the Southwest who inhabited these villages.

reservation—A tract of land set aside by treaty for the occupation and use of Indians. Some reservations were for an entire tribe; many others were for unaffiliated Indians.

Santa Fe Trail—A trade route between Independence, Missouri, and Santa Fe, New Mexico.

shaman—A priest who uses magic for the purpose of curing the sick, divining the hidden, and controlling events.

Sobaipuri—A Pima tribe of Native Americans living in the San Pedro and Santa Cruz river valleys.

tepee—A conical dwelling of the Plains tribes. It consists of a framework of circular poles brought together at the top and covered with animal hides.

treaty—A contract negotiated between representatives of the United States and one or more Indian tribes. Treaties dealt with surrender of political independence, peaceful relations, land sales, boundaries, and related matters.

tribe—A type of society consisting of a community or group of communities that occupy a common territory and are related by bonds of kinship, language, and shared traditions.

Ute—Part of the Shoshonean-speaking division of Native Americans who inhabited Colorado and portions of Utah.

White-painted Woman—Earth Mother. In Apache mythology, she is considered the mother of the Apaches.

wickiup—A brush shelter or mat-covered house used by southwestern Indians.

witch—A user of evil power.

Books

Aleshire, Peter. *Warrior Woman: The Story of Lozen, Apache Warrior and Shaman.* New York: St. Martin's Press, 2001.

Ball, Eve. *In the Days of Victorio.* Tucson, Ariz.: University of Arizona Press, 1970.

Barrett, S.M., ed. *Geronimo's Story of His Life.* New York: Irvington, 1983.

Basso, Keith H. *The Cibecue Apache.* New York: Holt, Rinehart and Winston, 1970.

Betzinez, Jason, and W.S. Nye. *I Fought with Geronimo.* New York: Bonanza Books, 1959.

Buskirk, Winfred. *The Western Apache.* Norman, Okla.: University of Oklahoma Press, 1986.

Cole, D.C. *The Chiricahua Apache, 1846–1876: From War to Reservation.* Albuquerque, N.M.: University of New Mexico Press, 1988.

Cremony, John C. *Life among the Apaches.* Glorieta, N.M.: Rio Grande Press, 1868 (1969).

Frantz, Klaus. *Indian Reservations in the United States.* Chicago, Ill.: University of Chicago Press, 1999.

Goodwin, Grenville. *The Social Organization of the Western Apache.* Chicago, Ill.: University of Chicago Press, 1942.

Griffith, A. Kinney. *The First Hundred Years of Nino Cochise: The Untold Story of an Apache Indian Chief,* as told by Ciye "Nino" Cochise to A. Kinney Griffith. New York: Abelard-Schuman, 1971.

Gunnerson, Dolores. *The Jicarilla Apaches: A Study in Survival.* DeKalb, Ill.: Northern Illinois University Press, 1974.

Hoijer, Harry. *Chiricahua and Mescalero Apache Texts*: Available online at *http://etext.lib.virginia.edu/apache/.*

Iverson, Peter. *We Are Still Here: American Indians in the Twentieth Century.* Wheeling, Ill.: Harlan Davidson, Inc., 1998.

Lockwood, Frank. *Pioneer Days in Arizona.* New York: Macmillan, 1932.

———. *The Apache Indians*. New York: n.p., 1938.

McKissack, Patricia C. *Run Away Home*. New York: Scholastic Paperbacks, 2001.

Melody, Michael E. *The Apaches: A Critical Bibliography*. Bloomington, Ind.: Indiana University Press, 1977.

Opler, Morris Edward. *An Apache Life-Way: The Economic, Social, and Religious Institutions of the Chiricahua Indians*. Chicago, Ill.: University of Chicago Press, 1941.

Perry, Richard J. *Apache Reservation: Indigenous Peoples and the American State*. Austin, Texas: University of Texas Press, 1993.

Roberts, David. *Once They Moved Like The Wind: Cochise, Geronimo, and the Apache Wars*. New York: Touchstone, 1994.

Stockel, H. Henrietta. *Shame & Endurance: The Untold Story of the Chiricahua Apache Prisoners of War*. Tucson, Ariz.: University of Arizona Press, 2004.

Terrell, John. *Apache Chronicle*. New York: World Publishing Co., 1972.

Tiller, Veronica. *The Jicarilla Apache Tribe*. Lincoln, Nebr.: University of Nebraska Press, 1983.

Waters, Frank. *Masked Gods*. New York: New York: Ballantine Books, 1950.

Watt, Eva Tulene, and Keith Basso. *Don't Let the Sun Step over You: A White Mountain Apache Family Life (1860–1976)*. Tucson, Ariz.: University of Arizona Press, 2004.

Websites

Chiricahua Apache Nation
http://www.chiricahuaapache.org/

Fort Sill Apache Tribe
http://www.fortsillapachenation.com/home.html

Jicarilla Apache Nation
http://www.jicarillaonline.com/

BIBLIOGRAPHY AND FURTHER READING

Mescalero Apache Reservation
http://www.mescaleronet.com/

Geronimo: His Own Story
http://odur.let.rug.nl/~usa/B/geronimo/geronixx.htm

San Carlos Apache Nation
http://www.sancarlosapache.com/home.htm

Handbook of Texas Online: The Apache Indians
http://www.tsha.utexas.edu/handbook/online/articles/view/AA/bma33.html

White Mountain Apache Tribe
http://www.wmat.nsn.us/

The Yavapai-Apache Nation
http://www.yavapai-apache.org/

PICTURE CREDITS

Michael E. Melody, Ph.D., is Professor of Political Science at Barry University in Miami Shores, Florida. He has published several books, including *The Apaches: A Critical Biography* and *The Apachean Cosmos.*

Paul C. Rosier received his Ph.D. in American History from the University of Rochester, with a specialty in Native American History. His first book, *Rebirth of the Blackfeet Nation, 1912–1954,* was published by the University of Nebraska Press in 2001. In November 2003, Greenwood Press published *Native American Issues* as part of its Contemporary American Ethnic Issues series. Dr. Rosier has also published articles on Native American topics in the *American Indian Culture and Research Journal,* and the *Journal of American Ethnic History.* In addition, he was coeditor of *The American Years: A Chronology of United States History.* He is Assistant Professor of History at Villanova University, where he also serves as a faculty advisor to the Villanova Native American Student Association.

Ada E. Deer is the director of the American Indian Studies program at the University of Wisconsin–Madison. She was the first woman to serve as chair of her tribe, the Menominee Nation, the first woman to head the Bureau of Indian Affairs in the U.S. Department of the Interior, and the first American Indian woman to run for Congress and secretary of state of Wisconsin. Deer has also chaired the Native American Rights Fund, coordinated workshops to train American Indian women as leaders, and championed Indian participation in the Peace Corps. She holds degrees in social work from Wisconsin and Columbia.